Is There Really Life After Death?

The Believer's Identification with Christ in His Death, Burial, and Resurrection

George K. Somerville, DPhil

an imprint of
GlobalEd AdvancePress

IS THERE REALLY LIFE AFTER DEATH?
The Believer's Identification with Christ in His Death, Burial, and Resurrection.

Library of Congress Control Number: 2009936518

Somerville, George K., 1934-
Is There Really Life After Death?

ISBN 978-1-935434-35-1
Subject Codes and Description:

1. REL012000: Religion: Christian Life - General
2. REL. 012040: Religion: Christian Life - Inspirational
3. REL 006980 Religion: Biblical Criticism and Interpretation

Cover design by Barton Green

Printed in the United States of America

Published by
Post-Gutenberg Books™
An Imprint of
GlobalEdAdvancePress

This book is dedicated to my wife, Shirley,

who remained faithful over the first twenty-five years,
became supportive over the latter twenty-five years,
and in whose honor this book was written.

I also wish to show gratitude to
Hollis L. Green, Th.D., Ph.D., and
Charles R. Solomon, Ed.D.,
for their editing insight for this book.

Table of Contents

Publisher's Foreword

Dr. George Somerville emphasized in this book that the resurrection of Christ can readily be confirmed through reading the scriptures. He shows how, we too, could experience the reality of resurrection glory. Those, who earnestly seek after Biblical Truth, will find that resurrected life is recognized as Christ's Eternal Life. Therefore, life after death can only be identified in Christ, confirmed in experience, and made real through that measure of imparted faith received upon salvation.

Throughout the book new life was identified as revival. The term revival was never meant to be an event happening outside the body. To live again was prefaced as being raised from the dead as a new creature. The old nature was discarded as flesh. In order to live again, something or some one had to die. In this case, it was the old man, the self, or the humanity of man. The nature of man, based in Adam, was crucified, and a new creature was created in exchange for the old. The new "me" is in Christ.

This new "me," according to Dr. Somerville, further identified the Christian as being in Christ. The death of Christ assured the believer of a place in resurrection. The Believer is placed into Christ's death, buried with Him in the tomb, and then raised with Him in Glory. The author demonstrated concern for the apathy within the church and showed how the clergy paints the creature as being positional, or in the state of being arranged, or as a provisional *status quo*. All too often they seek to obey the doctrines of the church rather than the doctrines of the Bible. The congregation needs sound theological teaching.

According to Dr. Somerville, the protestant reformation became established not so much as an act of faith, but as an act of charity by those who were tired of paying tribute to the Roman Church. It was an action of works rather than faith. Even though Martin Luther saw that justification by faith denied the need for a human mediator, it soon became the norm to come under a church composed of some community ethic and good works.

A community of grace is common to all Christians who confess Jesus Christ as Savior and Lord. It is true that many are conformist, and believe in an orthodox church, but to others it may not be an acceptable community. This book seeks to establish the basis and power of transformation to all who believe. The scripture warns Believers not to be conformed, but to be transformed by the renewing (restructuring) of the mind. (Romans 12:2)

When revival happens, people repent and are baptized into the death of Christ. It follows then, that if baptized into His death, you are buried, and raised again to new life in Christ. (Romans 6:3-6) Revival, throughout this book, was seen as resurrection glory. As you can see by the references there are many who take up the cross daily and follow Christ unto His death. Paul spoke strongly of this in his letter to the Philippians, and with that I say unto you, Good Day!

That I may know him, and the power of his resurrection, and the fellowship of his sufferings, being made conformable unto his death; if by any means I might attain unto the resurrection of the dead. Not as though I had already attained, either were already perfect: but I follow after, if that I may apprehend that for which also I am apprehended of Christ Jesus.
(Philippians 3:10-12)

Author's Preface

This book is about life after death. It is the result of nearly fifty years in the Christian faith. It is written from the knowledge and background that comes through humility and rejection. The book is developed from experiential data of living life in the resurrection. (Nee, 1972) The data and supportive literature was gathered over twenty-two years of research. Its source and structure are for ministry.

Any work, by which Church failure is an effect, is caused through denial of the deity of Christ. Using a version of the Bible that deletes or modifies a passage of scripture in the New Testament that speaks to the deity of Christ, can lead to denial of the Living Christ. According to statistics, fifty seven percent of evangelical Christians believe Jesus may not be the only way, or the absolute truth, that leads to eternal Life. Yet, according to the Scriptures, Jesus is the Way, the Truth, and the Life; no one comes to the Father except by Him. (John 14:6) Whenever the authority of the Word of God is over shadowed by humanistic and modern theology, faith will be compromised. Evolution, disagreement on election, and the functional operation of denominationalism deter the cause and effect of the Holy Spirit. This is the philosophy of existentialism, a process of reason leading to practicing the occult. (Young, 1963)

The book deals with a number of issues over the diversity of such practice. The question is asked if some of these practices are of God or Satan, or even as wolves dressed in sheep's clothing claiming to be angels of light. One must question the spirits if they are of God or Satan. Each person needs to know the drum to which they are marching. Are we marching after the flesh to the beat of a religious/political movement, or are we marching to the trumpet call of the Spirit in a halleluiah chorus? The Holy Spirit speaks quietly of Jesus of Nazareth, the only begotten Son of God. One who came without sin in the flesh; lived thirty-three years among men; was crucified, raised from the dead, and is ascended to the Father of Light in heaven.

The Church must have a Mandate

The Church, if it is to survive, must follow her mandate. She must be set free to preach the gospel, heal the brokenhearted, recover sight to the blind, and set at liberty those that are of a broken spirit. Jesus said, "Come unto me, all you who are heavy laden, and I will give you rest. Take my yoke upon you and learn of me; for I am meek and lowly in heart; come and find rest unto your souls; my yoke is easy, and my burden is light."(Matthew 11:28-30) The conversion experience is unique to the individual. If it cannot be established within the context of scripture, it should be questioned for authenticity.

The Gospel directive is authentic in relationship. The Deity of Jesus is confirmed in the Christian. The Lord pours out His Spirit on all who call upon His name. No one can deny the power of the resurrected life in experience. Founded on the fact that God raised Jesus Christ from the dead, we too are raised to a glorified life. This is resurrection. The subsequent hope of every Christian then, is the physical redemption of a glorified body. (Ephesians 1:13-14)

However, the new "me" in Christ began in resurrection. John the Baptist said of Jesus, "Behold the Lamb of God that takes away the sin of the world." Isaac asked of his father Abraham, "Behold the wood and the fire, but where is the Lamb for a burnt offering? My son, God will provide Himself a Lamb." (Genesis 22: 5-8) God came, prepared as a Lamb for the slaughter, and dwelt on earth as Jesus of Nazareth. He prepared a body of flesh and blood. This same body was slain as a sin offering on a cursed wooden tree. His blood, a perfect sacrifice, was shed for all humanity. Whosoever follows Him in death, and believes He took the judgment of God for their sin, becomes the righteousness of God in Christ.

Israel, the elect, according to the foreknowledge of God the Father, is set apart and made Holy unto obedience by the blood of Jesus Christ. This act brings together the promises of God to Abraham, and in effect, to bear unto all those who would call upon His Name, whether Jew or Gentile, pass from death unto life. (John 5:24)

The body of Christ on the cross does not give life. He was stricken dead! The only sign given for resurrected life is the sign of Jonah. After three days God took Jonah from the belly of a fish. After three days, God brought forth Jesus out from the grave. Resurrected life is the sign of Jonah. It was the only sign Jesus gave to His adversaries. The people of Nineveh repented and believed. Even so,

God raised Jesus from the dead that we might receive life everlasting in the glory of His resurrection.

Christ ascended to heaven, but before lift off, He promised to return for His Bride, the Church. The day approaches of His imminent return. Jesus was literally raised from the dead in a glorified body. How marvelous, that we should be placed into His death that we might be components of that Body. We are raised together with Christ, and live as spiritual creatures. While yet in heavenly places at the right hand of God the Father, Jesus will honor His promise, that we too, shall have a redeemed, immortal, and incorruptible body. Even so, come Lord Jesus. (Ephesians 1:13, 2:6)

These things are all explained in the Book of Genesis, the four Gospels, the Letters of the Prophets, and epistles to the Apostles. Believe that Jesus is the Christ, and that all authority is given Him of the Father. Until all these things are restored, we faithfully wait in the promise, not with a compromising theory of institutionalism, but with the hope and faith of a loving Savior who bore our sins on the cross, that we might exchange them for new life in Christ.

Introduction

The New Creature in Christ

The book explains the spiritual view of what happens in the Believer at salvation. This, in confirmation of new life after death, is eternal life. Many trust the church for their salvation. It does not happen in the church; it happens in the Believer. After twenty-five years serving the Church, I experienced life after death, otherwise known as a spiritual awakening. I then conducted comparative research within the framework of church renewal and the Holy Spirit. Today, I counsel from the insight revealed through that experience. Until you come under the direction of the Holy Spirit in dealing with the flesh or self-life, what I share with you may lead to your spiritual awakening.

The evangelical church has failed in keeping the door open to scriptural illumination. The door that extended the right hand of fellowship to Believers is all but lost to a wide world of entertainment. Being welcomed, other than as an observer, is lacking in most churches. It is as if the seeker of truth is laden with germs. Resurrected life after death admits to a theological bias. What one brings to the congregation should be freedom through acceptance in the bond of peace, but never in rejection of experience.

The word renewal is lost in a myriad of experience. It means, "to live again" and implies a revived life. In his letter to the Roman church, Paul claims to have been alive once before the law. Paul experienced a former life, a reference to being in Adam. Paul experienced a sinless existence. When the law came, sin came to life (revived) and he died. While yet in the Loins of Adam, Paul was no longer free to serve and worship God. In Adam, Paul was inflicted by shame and placed in bondage to sin. This led to a life without conscience and communion. (Romans 7:9)

God had decreed a law that said, "You shall not eat of the fruit of the knowledge of good and evil." (Genesis 2:17) Sin indeed, raised its ugly head, and Paul, while yet in the loins of Adam, yielded to the sin of disobedience. The sin of disobedience destroys the effect of righteousness. If believers are to grow and mature in righteousness, they cannot be at war with the law of sin in the flesh.

Many churches do not explain the origin of sin. The effect of sin is manifested in the flesh, but the origin of sin was in Adam. Only in Christ, is one released from the bondage of sin. Many Christians think they are sinners saved by grace. After going forward time and time again confessing sin that manifest itself through the flesh, Christians remain in bondage to Adam's sin of disobedience. Being in Adam, one cannot be set apart from the bondage of sin. Salvation implies that Christ bore the judgment imposed upon Adam. Christ redeemed us from the curse that lay within. In that He died unto sin once, we too, die unto sin once. The stain that separates saint from sinner is the blood of Christ. Being raised together with Christ, believers are set free from sin, and secured in Christ, (Rom. 6:9-11; Eph. 2:5-9)

The Wedge

There is a wedge of indifference between the saint and the sinner who is compromised by an institutionalized church. Indifference is the state of mediocrity. We are only human is an excuse many give for their indulgence in sin. The cause of being "born again" has the effect of separation, a cure for the sin of indulgence. Most churches practice tolerance, unless proven to be heresy. This wedge separates the saint from the sinner and creates denominational bias. The doctrine of original sin and the judgment for sin are over looked. It is an indulgence for sin. Jesus Christ, who knew no sin, became sin for us, and bore the wrath of God's Judgment on our behalf. (Mathew 26:38-45) The saint is set free in Christ from the bondage of original sin.

The church member who follows after the flesh is tolerant of sin, and excuses it as being a human weakness. The judgment of God's wrath rested on Christ. The judgment of Adam's posterity is crucified on the cross. (Galatians 2:20) The spirit of the new creation is raised together in Christ Jesus. The wedge that separates the saint and sinner nullifies the effects of the cross. It compares to that of Martin Luther who nailed ninety five theses to the door of the All Saint's Church for the practice of selling indulgences in tolerance of those in purgatory. There is no further sacrifice for sin. Jesus, died unto sin once, is alive unto God. He cannot be crucified again.
(Romans 6:10)

New age teaching is the epitome of this wedge of indifference. Tolerance and deliberation of sin has all but dignified sin in the flesh, even to the renunciation of the deity of Christ. The church has come under the influence of an unobtrusive style of music. Using both acoustic and electronic instruments they draw on classical music, jazz, and rock. Under the influence some experience love, joy, peace, and support; others experience confusion, division, heartache, and denial. How much is too much?

Many local churches have accepted this trend. No questioning of the psychological effects of a musical chant that lead to chaos, and perhaps even demonic activity. Rather than singing psalms, hymns, and spiritual songs with grace in their hearts to the Lord, they jump, holler, and dance in the aisles of the churches. Who can hear the still quiet voice of the Spirit in such meetings? Is this the prompting of the Holy Spirit, or an unholy spirit enticing the rhythms of a darkened flesh?

The foundation of the Church is breaking apart. The doctrine of original sin has survived all the philosophies of man and is critical to the establishment of the Church. Unless original sin is dealt with on the cross, the saint remains a sinner, and is yet to be saved by grace. Thus, sin has compromised the deity of Christ. This progressive act opens the door to a religious/political movement wherein Christ is not recognized.

The Revived Structure

This book does not support religious leaders who deny Jesus died and rose again the third day. It is a book for those interested in victorious Christian living. Victorious Christians identify with new life in the Spirit. New life is not to be identified with a new confession, miracles, signs, or wonders; it is to be recognized as a new creation. The doctrine of justification affects the new creature in Christ. However, since the Christian's hope is based on the resurrection of Jesus Christ, a new generation of creatures is already in place. If resurrection, the sign of Jonas be denied, (Luke 11:29-30) Christ's deity is denied, and all hope is lost. If Christians base their faith on confession, they have yet to identify with Christ in His death, burial, and resurrection. Believers are the first fruits of the gospel, and after the church is removed, those who are Christ's at his coming. (I Corinthians 15:12-28)

This book presents a hope for a Christian awakening. With a background of experience, literature, and historical research, this work is the result of Christian experience, counsel, and knowledge of the exchanged life. The Believer is redeemed by the blood of Christ, the supreme sacrifice that sets us free from the bondage of sin. We have confidence, that since Christ became sin for us, we have become the righteousness of God in Him. (2 Corinthians 5:21) Read the book, listen with your heart, and read the references in a King James Bible.

Lord willing, you have identified with Resurrected life after death. This book provides additional research and supportive documentation for you to dig deeper into the reality of being in Christ's Eternal Life. Abide in Christ; experience His abundant Life. Chapter one begins with a cause for revival. May God bless as you read, study, and meditate upon its contents.

Chapter One

Resurrection Confirmed

The Witness

The resurrected life after death assumes the reality of the physical resurrection of Jesus Christ. This is the Christian's hope. The source, out of which Christianity emerged collectively, begins with the Baptism of John, and progresses unto the day Jesus ascended to heaven. Mary Magdalene, the one who learned at the feet of Jesus, was the first witness of the resurrected Lord. The witness of the resurrected Christ is glorified in the sight of man. The disciples witnessed the ascension of the resurrected Christ. Paul witnessed the ascended resurrected Christ on the Damascus road. The Spirit, bearing witness with our spirit, stands in witness to the experiential reality of our resurrected life in Christ.

Living the Resurrected Life is a spiritual journey. The pristine New Testament written for believers stands in contrast to the modern versions. The life of Jesus Christ His death, burial and resurrection all give testimony to the deity of a resurrected Lord. The authority given to man can be counted as nothing, when compared to Christ in resurrection. This mystery among the Gentiles is known through the measure of faith given by the risen Christ. This is confirmation of faith as the gift of God. It is for those who trust God, and believe His written Word.

Faith is imparted, under the authority of resurrection, to those who believe. Doubt is an instrument of reason. Worry is the medium of doubt. There is no questioning of the authority of God in resurrection when confirmed by His measure of faith given those in Christ.

The Fellowship

The fellowship of His resurrection is made known through the measure of faith given through the risen Christ. Fellowship and suffering are congruent in experience. Fellowship in resurrection can only be experienced under the authority of Christ. This is the way to follow Jesus. Faith becomes operational in resurrection life. Faith is the process by which believers are placed into the resurrected life. We function as the Holy Spirit quickens our mortal body, and communicates with the soul, or personality.

Functionisdependentonspiritualdirection.Anindividual's initial purpose before the Lord is to acknowledge the old nature (self) as crucified, and in exchange, place Christ's divine nature (Holy Spirit) in control. Except an individual surrender self to the authority of the Holy Spirit, they cannot know the resurrected life that follows after the will of God. The Holy Spirit imparts the measure of faith to believe by bringing Christ's life into union with the new creation. This is accomplished through the operation of faith given by the risen Christ. As Christ is destined to be King of Kings and Lord of Lords, even so, the Christian is destined to have fellowship with Christ in a resurrected life. Yes, there is life after death.

The Suffering

To have contempt for those things that are past, presses the Christian toward the cross. Grasp or lay hold on the things that mark the pathway of the high calling of God in Christ Jesus. These are made known through that measure of faith given by the risen Christ. Therefore, as many are of this leading so yield the complete self, and become followers together in the pattern of resurrection.

To grieve is to weep after the sadness of the Spirit for those Christians who walk after the flesh. Destined for defeat outside the experience of resurrected life, they consistently confess, and look unto Jesus for more compassion. They seek to renew their vows by placing Jesus back on the cross that greater forgiveness may be shown. This confession is a work of the flesh, and brings frustration to the soul, and so grieves the Holy Spirit. Works of the flesh become god, in whose glory is their shame yet beholding earthly things in the tabernacle of sin.

The Assurance

Prayer brings assurance on earth, and so interacts in the embodiment of resurrected glory. It is from within this embodiment of resurrection the Christian relates to Christ. The Christian looks unto the Lord Jesus Christ in anticipation that he/she shall emerge in victory over a degenerate body, and be fashioned like unto Christ's glorious resurrected body. This is according to the instrument of faith given by the risen Christ. The Christian rests in the confidence by which Jesus brings all things unto Himself for presentation to the Father.

Many scripture references are given in this book. Let there be no misunderstanding between the physical resurrection of the body and that of the resurrected new creature in Christ. The new creation is in Christ in heavenly places whereas the body of the Christian is the temple of the Holy Spirit on earth. God's only begotten whom He appointed heir of all things, by whom He made the worlds, unites the Christian with the Father in resurrection. Jesus Christ, the express image of the Father, sits at the right hand of Majesty. We are raised together with Christ.

The Reality

Many Christians, upon reading this for the first time, may find the teaching of the resurrected life experience difficult to comprehend. You may even dismiss it as impossible. Let no one be so bold as to think they have privileged information. God is not a respecter of persons. The teaching of a spiritual resurrection for the believer is not a new thought, but is an identity of the divine life in Christ.

Paul, when he addressed the Athenians at Mars Hill, ran across a similar stumbling block. As it was then so it is today, the question of deity is in the reality of resurrection. Those who are new to the Christian faith, and those mature to the faith, come unto the Living Stone to be broken. The Stone, a metaphor of the Christ, rejected of man, but of God, is chosen and precious. Christians are living stones, chosen and precious in the sight of God, a spiritual house, a holy priesthood, acceptable to God in Christ, and abound in resurrection glory.

Christ, the chief corner stone, chosen, and precious, and the Christian who believes, should not be troubled when they learn they are also chosen and precious. The truth of who the Christian is in Christ is to believe in resurrected spiritual life after death. Should there be no resurrection for Christ, peace and hope for the Christian is lost. Do not doubt the authority of the Christian faith.

The Evolution of Progression

Repentance is the baptism of John. God launched Christ's three-year ministry in His baptism by John. He went into the waters identified as the son of man, and rose from the waters identified as the Son of God, and seen as the Lamb of God. (John 1:34-36) His ministry of sacrifice was fulfilled in His death, burial, and resurrection. The cause of repentance, the baptism of John, is to effect salvation. That which places doubt in the mind of the believer concerning the Deity of Christ, and the authenticity of the Word of God, affects the resurrected life. Doubt, being an instrument of reason and medium of worry, is an effect of progressive thought resulting in mysticism giving way to the notion there are many ways to heaven. Christ's ministry, confirmed by the descending Holy Ghost, whose will it is, to return with the living Church of God. (2 Thessalonians 2:7)

Evolution is the theory of progression among living species. Compared with creation, man evolved over time in patterns of greater and greater complexity. A Christian matures out of who they are in Christ, not of how well they perform. Progressive sanctification is an evolving concept. Believers emerge from infancy to adulthood. Their history is monitored through the hope and anticipation of a physical resurrection. Maturity can be analyzed based on known experiences in life. The foreknowledge of God, in the baptism of Jesus, attests to the validity of the resurrection. Believers do not move progressively to eternity, believers abide in Christ.

The new creature is spirit, embodied in Christ, in resurrection, and in heavenly places. The Christian, to live in victory in community is serviced by anticipation, the hope of resurrection. The chosen one is destined to experience death, burial, and resurrection. In an instant, one is made a new creature in Christ. Revival is not some evolving crisis experience, but rising from the dead, we give witness concerning victory in the resurrected Christ, and provide lasting assurance in the hope of salvation.

The Maturity

Maturity demands that believers know who they are in Christ. The Holy Bible in its original format is not available, but the inspired Word of God is for everyone. Were we to study, as directed, one would need to have the original. It is imperative for a Christian to believe God has the authority to preserve His Word. Many believe the King James Bible is a reliable English Bible. Knowledge of who we are in Christ, acknowledged before God and man, and having received the measure of faith, we accept the fact of the resurrection experience. Believers must accept the Bible as the Living Word of God.

When an individual fails to validate the Word of God through experiential truth and chooses not to accept the faith given those in Christ in resurrection, repentance is unlikely. Continual confession is to crucify the Son of God afresh, and put Christ to open shame. Maturity in the Word of God is not validated through feelings, signs, wonders, and fantasy, but in the knowledge of God through persistent obedience to the law of God in Christ.

The Repentance

The first emotion felt by Adam and Eve was shame. Shame evolved into blame resulting in bondage of mankind to the will of the flesh. Worry or anxiety evolved into fear of exposure, fear evolved into deception, and deception is the denial of knowledge. The Word of God leads the Christian into knowledge, repentance, and into a living hope. There is no judgment pending the Christian who abides in Christ Jesus, and walk victoriously in the Spirit.

Repentance brings about the emergence of new life in the Spirit for the believer. God made Jesus to be wisdom, righteousness, sanctification, and redemption, and placed Him as the pattern of resurrected life. The question was never "what" is a Christian but rather "who" is Christian. The Believer who abides in Christ and manifests Christ's Life in resurrection has become Christ-like. Repentance develops the mystery of the Believer in Christ. It is evidence of resurrected life after death.

The Believer is saved by faith. Hope provides patience in waiting for the fulfillment of hope in physical resurrection. The more accurately the Christian applies the Scriptures to the inner man, the more illumination they receive by the Spirit. Modern syntax, grammar, and punctuation, has made a profound difference in reading the Bible, but in all the translations, versions, and paraphrases, one should attempt to read the epistles (letters) in first person singular. The epistles, are letters to the saints, and are written to, for, and about the Saints. The epistles confirm the faithful to be in Christ as children of God living in resurrection glory.

This book was written from the viewpoint of one awakened to new life in Christ. Awakened to the need for experiential knowledge; it is an approach to assist the Church in bringing about an awakening to the Body of Christ. God imparts foolish thoughts to perplex the mind of the wise: God imparts weak thoughts to baffle the mighty; God imparts important thoughts, rejected thoughts, and light thoughts to the reasoning mind, so no flesh could glory in His presence. God is omnipresent, omnipotent, and omniscient. God's Living Word is for those who would bring glory to the Lord. This book is in testimony of the author's personal identification with the Lord in resurrection life.

Humility in Resurrection

Humility is the state or quality of being set free from pride and arrogance; a lowliness of mind; a modest estimate of one's worth; a sense of one's unworthiness; and self-abasement. Paul served the Lord with humility of mind. In a humble manner, he boldly asserted the cause of Christ. He warned about walking in or after the flesh, and the futility of contending in the flesh for the cause of righteousness. He put his confidence in the new creation, and made it clear how the flesh is jealous, and at war with the Holy Spirit. The Spirit is also jealous of the flesh. Paul's emphasis was on those who have crucified the flesh. Emotions, with the affections and lusts, reveal the sinfulness of the flesh. This is not humility, but pride. The saying, "I'm only a sinner saved by grace" is the epitome of a proud and boastful heart. There is no pride in those who live and reveal the fruit of the Spirit.

On the Damascus road, Paul met the ascended Christ in His resurrected body. Immediately, Paul recognized the authority of God by asking, "Who art thou Lord?" He was shown the error of his way and humbled himself before the risen Christ. To experience humility, to be free from sin, one must be broken through death on the cross.

Advancing humanity is conceptual. A framework, by which the religious ethic of Felix Adler felt the church had failed as a religious community is called humanistic. Christian counselors, in their ethic of being professional, often conform to a reasoning mind from which comes vanity. To reason from a "positional" stance of Christianity, is conceptualism.

Counselees seek justification of self. This is an excuse for their actions. Counselors have great difficulty dividing the soul and spirit. It is clear from the scriptures that the Living Word of God divides the soul and spirit into different components. This truth shows how fallen man's old spirit is the very nature of Adam. It is the fallen nature, the self, flesh, or old man that is crucified with Christ. Admitting the nature of man as fallen is one thing, but to admit the fact that the fallen nature of man must be crucified is an admission of true humility.

The Flesh

Resentment, envy, strife, backstabbing, and defeat are the characteristics of carnal (fleshly) Christians. To live victoriously in Christ Jesus, is not according to how well one can battle the flesh. If the Christian is to battle from within the flesh, where then is the Holy Spirit? The battle for the mind is not a physical battle, but a spiritual battle. The weapons deployed cannot be fashioned from things that are earthy, but from things that are in heaven. True humility is submitting to the power of God, pulling down every stronghold of reason, and acknowledging the word of God. The weapons of spiritual warfare are spiritually discerned.

The Spiritual Warfare

Salvation is complete. Christ brought about salvation through spiritual warfare. It was not without loss and suffering. To live again in Christ, is the experiential power of the resurrection. As children of God, believers overcome, and have victory through that Life who overcame the world. Through faith, given us in Christ Jesus, believers are raised together in Christ. The concern is how believers attack the strongholds that hinder Christians from living in harmony. A song of David declared, Behold, how good and how pleasant it is for brethren to dwell together in unity.

Paul said, “I therefore, the prisoner of the Lord, beseech you that you walk worthy of the vocation wherewith you are called, with all lowliness, and meekness, with longsuffering, forbearing one another in love: Endeavoring to keep the unity of the Spirit in the bond of peace: . . . Christ, when He ascended, led captivity captive, and gave gifts unto men: . . . For the perfecting of the Saints; for the work of ministry; for the edifying of the Body of Christ; till we all come in the unity of the faith, unto a perfect man. This measure is of the stature, and fullness of Christ. We henceforth are no longer children, tossed to and fro, carried about with winds of doctrine, by the sleight (deceitfulness) of men, and cunning craftiness, whereby they lie in wait to deceive." (Ephesians 4:1-32)

Spiritual warfare is beyond the control of a carnal mind. A stronghold is a garrison fortified to protect a defending arsenal. It may be a big gun or a trench filled with armed soldiers. There are strongholds of mind that Christians must overcome if they are to know Christ, the power of His resurrection, His fellowship, His sufferings, and being made conformable unto His death, His Eternal Life. The Christian conducts an offensive attack on behalf of an efficacious Cross.

It is before the Cross, whereby the enemy has set strongholds of the mind. No one wants to entertain death. Yet, death is for real. One can experience new life in resurrection only through the death of self. Being placed into the death of Christ, believers are buried, and raised unto new life in resurrection. Resurrected Life after death is only available through Christ's suffering, his crucifixion. Defeat is the effect of a reasoning mind. Victory is the effect of the Holy Spirit, in the power of resurrection.

The Offense

Paul, in Romans Chapter Seven, wrote of his warfare against strongholds of the mind. After all the attempts are exhausted, he asks, “O wretched man that I am! Who shall deliver me from this body of death?” In defeat, it appears that even Paul succumbed to images portrayed on a fleshly mind. There is no victory. Must the Christian live out life on earth in defeat?

This is not victory. A Christian, who appropriates their co-death, co-burial, co-resurrection, and co-ascension in Christ asks, “O death where is your sting: O grave where is your victory?” It is gone! “The sting of death is sin, and the strength of sin is law.” Christian, the secret to victory is your death, burial, and resurrection in Christ.

Many pastors see Romans Chapter Seven as an excuse to cover their ignorance of the power of sin in the flesh. If you keep on confessing your sins week after week, month after month, and year after year, you become dependent on the pastor or priest to hear your sin. They are, in reality, co-dependent. If the confessionals were no longer in existence, how would your pastor or priest function, let alone represent the church in community?

The Christian should, as Paul did in humility, give thanks to God for deliverance from this body of death. Paul knew, from Romans chapter six, this body of death (sin) is destroyed. (Romans 6:6) The strongholds of the mind are consistently brought to the conscience, but are no longer effective. In the righteousness of God, we have victory in Christ to serve the law of God. The law of God is fulfilled in Christ. Be aware, the flesh serves the law of sin. Those who follow after the flesh will to serve the law of sin. It is a choice. Repentance in humility is victory.

There are two sources of power from which to choose. One, the power of the Mind of Christ who indwells through obedience to the law of God, or two, the power of indwelling sin which empowers through obedience to the law of sin. It is a matter of the will. But, that's not all! Recall how, in the Garden of Eden, the serpent, indwelt by the sin of inequity, overcame and brought Adam and Eve into captivity by lies: God said, "You Shall not eat of the tree of the knowledge of good and evil, else you will die." The serpent said, "You will not die, but you will become as gods." This tactic of lies is still being used today by those who would destroy the Church. They appeal to our mind of reason.

When a thought or action is being considered, it can be given over to disobedience by reason, or it can be given over to the knowledge of God and through obedience to Christ have it destroyed. "Surely, God will not let you die." Eve began to ponder the thought, and in disobedience, took the fruit, ate, and gave to her husband Adam. This is the law of sin. What if there were no law? Would there be any need for judgment? Paul claims to be alive once without the law, while yet in the loins of Adam.

Every thought, good or evil that comes to the natural mind is of the flesh. They come as unrestrained passions, material possessions coveted by the eyes, or the vanity of a narcissistic life style. Reason is not of the Father, it is of the world, and the world passes away. Even Christ did not consider the suffering of the cup (God's wrath) or the baptism (His death) on the Cross of significant importance to reason, but chose the Father's will. It is better to be obedient to the will of God, than test His sovereignty over world events. It seems the fleshly mind is always open to vanity, imagination, and temptation.

The Kingdom of God is not open to those who are tempted to reason in the vanity of their mind. Thoughts that evoke envy, strife, and unfairness, lead to question the will of God. "Why me?" may be the result of the wrath of God upon disobedience.

Prisoners in Christ

Concerning the order of the resurrection, Jesus led captivity captive at His ascension. Paul claims he was a prisoner of the Lord. Was he referring to physical imprisonment because of ministry, or does he mean spiritual imprisonment in resurrection? The words imply a physical prison, but in context of a spiritual resurrection, captivity seems to be of a spiritual order.

In ascension, Jesus took captivity captive to heaven those who he preached to in prison and those who are placed into His death on the cross. Our co-death, co-burial, and co-resurrection, includes co-ascension. The thief, to whom He promised paradise, was in the captivity; the spirits to whom he preached were in captivity, and we who are placed into His death are among the captivity. Paul, Epaphras, Christians past and present, are all fellow prisoners in Christ.

To be placed into Christ's death is to nullify the factor of time. There are no clocks in eternity. Faith provides us the substance by which we can believe these things, and is the evidence of things not seen. Resurrected life after death is all-sufficient in the measure of faith to believers. These concepts will not be realized until we go that way, and then, they will not be important.

Being raised to new life implies believing men, women, boys, and girls are placed into Christ's death. All inherit a future eternal life, and all inherit a life in eternity past. Since Christ is Eternal, those in Christ have a new past and a new future. In consideration of that awesome disposition, believers are enabled through faith, to comprehend their co-crucifixion, co-burial, co-resurrection, and co-ascension in Christ. This teaching is unique within Christianity as a whole.

The Religion of Self

Humanism is the religion of self; it is the enemy of God. Whosoever wills to put self-esteem before God, self is the enemy of God. The fallen spirit of Adam gives allegiance to the presence of iniquity; that is, sin dwelling in the flesh. It is envious, critical of others, and gives glory to the self. Pride is of self; a friend of the world. When compared with a believer, who by God's grace receives the humility of Christ, it is a fearful thing.

A person will question authority if led to believe something is being held back. Satan gave Eve reason to question God's command. Eve, seeing how the tree was good for food, reasoned with the mind. She did not listen, nor gave credence to her knowledge of God's law. She thought He was holding back information as to why the fruit was forbidden. How quickly, when thoughts cause one to reason against the knowledge of God, they become a stronghold of Satan.

The Secret of Victory

Choice is a function of the will. Paul claims "I, my inner self" serve the law of God, but the flesh serves the law of sin. The will holds the key to victory. The influence of the world and Satan cause the Christian to lean on their significant others in relationship. They cause one to be dependent. I, my inner self will linger for affirmation. If in obedience, there is no delay. The mind will yield to influence or rely on past experience. The benefit of serving the law of God is freedom from condemnation. The blood of Jesus is the veil by which the Christian boldly enters into the Holiest. It is by this new and living way that Jesus, in resurrection, is glorified.

The secret to victory is dependent upon bringing thoughts in line with the Word of God. The weapons of the Christian's warfare are not of the flesh, but mighty through God to the pulling down of strong holds. Casting down imaginations, and every high thought that exalts itself against the knowledge of God, bring each thought in captivity to the obedience of Christ: having in readiness to avenge all disobedience, obedience is fulfilled in Christ Jesus. This passage, taken literally, applied immediately, will destroy thoughts, or satanic influence upon the mind. This is one of the most powerful weapons for the cause of victory.

The Christian, in obedience to Christ, will not allow hostile thoughts to linger. In the power of resurrection they will to capture, and choose to bring them to the obedience of Christ. Upon letting to the Lord Jesus, He rejects or accepts them. It is His choice. Victory, herein described, is an empirical truism. It is evidenced by a peaceful return to sleep. The significance of the thought process should never be taken lightly, for spiritual warfare is all about who is in control, the law of God, or the law of sin.

The Simplicity

The simplicity that is in Christ confounds the wisdom of man. These things the world despises because they oppose the power of reason. Foolish things of the world are chosen of God to confound the wise; and weak things of the world are chosen to confound the mighty, that no reasoning of the flesh should glory in His presence. God is omnipresent. The Christian is the Temple of God. The tri-unity of man testifies to the fact that man is a three part being. The Christian identifies with the Holy Spirit in the spirit, who communes with the soul the thoughts of Christ, who manifests the character of Christ Jesus through the body. There is no extra biblical insight.

To know authority, is to obey the will of God. A Christian wills to process thoughts under the control of the Holy Spirit. When the Christian learns to trust in Jesus, whose authority cannot be usurped, he gives ascension to Christ's corporate control, God is glorified. If true, the Christian's imagination is under the control of the Holy Spirit. Satan's strong holds are destroyed; thoughts contrary to the knowledge of God are in captivity, given over to the obedience of Christ, they are judged accordingly.

The Sensitivity

Sensitivity is the by-product of compassion. Jesus tells the story of the Good Samaritan. The story is about a man who was robbed, left naked, and beaten nearly to death by a band of thieves. While on the side of the road, a Priest and a Levite came along, looked upon the man, and chose to pass by on the other side. Later, a Samaritan happened to come along who had compassion on the man. He then dressed his wounds, took him to an Inn, paid for his shelter, and anything else that was needed, he offered to pay. Jesus asked, "Which of these three is the good neighbor?" The answer, of course, came back to be the Samaritan. With that, Jesus told the lawyer to go and do likewise. Sensitivity to the need of another can be an act of compassion, but if it leads to false humility; the pride of serving; then it serves the law of sin in the flesh.

The Rejection Syndrome

The things of the world influence a Christian. Being sensitive to your neighbor in love denies the right to self, but when feelings toward others harden, insensitivity turns to rejection. Is there anything more disturbing than being ignored? A man was robbed, beaten, and left for dead on the side of the road. Rejection took precedence in three out of four examples.

Hurt can be physical, emotional, or spiritual. It is known

by symptoms of rejection. Rejection is being refused membership in a group; denied recognition for accomplishment; a feeling of despair. Rejection is experienced when told one is incompetent, unworthy, or out of place. Many Christians can attest to feeling inferior, insecure, inadequate, which lead to false guilt, worry, doubts, and phobia. The Christian has the characteristics of Adam's fallen race. Mankind suffers the effects of original sin, and being cast from Paradise, even feel rejected from the presence of God.

Blaming others does not resolve rejection. A new identity is difficult to accept. Except a kernel of grain fall into the ground and die it is rejected; but if it yields to death, it brings forth fruit. He that loves life shall lose it, and he that denies life shall keep it unto eternal life. To overcome the rejection syndrome, believers must deny self-daily and follow Jesus. The Christian abides in Christ. Jesus gave His life, that His eternal life may be received of many. This is the Grace of God, His unmerited favor, upon which we qualify in acceptance.

The Refreshment

In acceptance, God committed to believers the word of reconciliation. As citizens of heaven, He delegates the Christian as an ambassador. Dear brothers and sisters in the Lord, we have died to the law of sin and death; we are in union with the risen Christ; as chaste virgins, we bear fruit unto God. Surely, Jesus ascended into heaven, above all principality, power, and might, and dominion, and every name that is named, not only in this world, but in the world to come. Therefore, God has put all things under His control, and gave Him to be in charge of His body, the Church. Jesus is in the fullness of the Godhead. Being raised with Christ in resurrection, we attend to things that are above. The Christian is the everlasting glory of Christ. God quickens our mortal body; its members are deployed to carry the message of the Gospel to the world.

The Identity

God's Church is in the spiritual body of the living Christ. The Christian is chaste and undefiled by the world. The Church is identified by theology in denominational practice. Jesus Christ, according to the revelation of the mystery kept secret since the world began; made manifest by the scriptures of the prophets, and thus made known for obedience to the faith. (Romans 16:25, 26)

The spiritual Body of Christ was never intended to be the habitat of man. Those who would feed upon the carcasses of the prophets, apostles, Disciples of Christ, and naive' Christians are unable to endure sound teaching of the Word. Many, with itching ears, puffed up in vanity, follow headlong after false teachers. These teachers turn those with itching ears away from the truth and the inerrancy of God's Word into fables, and heresy.

The Obedience

The Lord Jesus, who is the Author and Finisher of the faith who, for the joy that was set before Him, endured the cross, despised the shame, and after it was fulfilled, sat down at the right hand of the Majesty. (Heb. 12:2) Jesus shares with us from personal experience, how it feels to be rejected? The Son of God, who being in the form of God, thought it not robbery to be equal with God: but made Himself of no reputation, and took upon Himself the form of a servant, and was made in the likeness and fashion of men, He humbled Himself, and became obedient unto death, even the death of the cross. (Phil. 2:8)

If any will to follow Jesus to the cross, then let him deny self, by taking up his cross daily. Isaiah the prophet said, "The people hear, but do not understand; they see, but do not perceive." Close your eyes, hear with your ears and understand with your heart, what Christ Jesus, through Paul, is saying in truth. The individual, through death, is become betrothed as His bride. Paul said to the Corinthian Church, "I love you, and I am jealous over you with a Godly jealousy: but I fear that your entanglement with the world, even as the serpent deceived Eve from obedience, your minds too, are become corrupted from the simplicity that is in Christ."

This chapter emphasized that the resurrection of Christ can readily be confirmed through reading the scriptures. It showed how, we too, could experience the reality of resurrection glory. Those, who earnestly seek after Biblical Truth, will find that resurrected life is recognized as Christ's Eternal Life. Therefore, life after death can only be identified in Christ, confirmed in experience, and made real through that measure of imparted faith received upon salvation. The next chapter, Preface to New Life, is an introduction to the revival experience. Written in preparation for the New Life.

Chapter Two

Preface to New Life

In The Beginning

Revival, as referred to in Church meetings, normally changes its definition, and the contextual use of the word. Revival is from two Latin words "re" meaning again, and "vivo" meaning to live; therefore the actual meaning is, "to live again." Applied spiritually, the natural life in Adam is exchanged for spiritual life in Christ. (1 Corinthians 15: 45-49) A change of attitude is not sufficient. Attitude is changing habits, and implies mixing the old with the new. A new patch should never be fixed to old material.

A pseudo revival is sweeping the nation. This revival calls for more confession, but without repentance. The Believer is saved through faith not by works. Revival is not an experience of confession, but rather, it is identification with Christ in His death, burial, resurrection, and ascension to heaven. (Romans 6:3-6) Resurrected life in Christ cannot be experienced until the old life in Adam is crucified: That life that first began in the Garden of Eden.

Pickers (choosers) of Good and Evil Fruit

Adam and Eve were fruit pickers. However, before they

were pickers, they were observers. The fruit looked good, and was to be eaten except from one lonely tree in the middle of the garden: the fruit of the knowledge of good and evil. This fruit was not for man's consumption, but a test of obedience that was set before man. However, upon observation, it was good for food, it was pleasant to the eye, and it was a fruit to be desired. And it was a test.

Eve knew the fruit was forbidden. Deceived, she picked it, ate it, and in transgression of the law, gave some to her husband Adam. They ate of the forbidden fruit in spite of knowing the consequences. In an instant, sin got the upper hand. Sin was revived, risen from the clutches of the serpent to exercise its power and intimidation over the creature. This time, it was taken up (revived) by man's lust for knowledge, and to be as little gods, knowing good and evil. Adam and Eve were put out from the Garden of Eden. They were to till the ground from which they were formed. (Genesis 3:22-24 and 1Timothy 2:14)

Sin was to live again (revived) in Adam. Sin was found in Lucifer and the King of Tyrus. (Isaiah 14:12-14; Ezekiel 28:12-15) Paul the Apostle, and mankind as a whole, in so much as we were in the loins of Adam, this sin of inequity, passed to generation upon generation. We, as fruit pickers, tillers of the soil, and pharmaceutical marvels through procreation, came short of the Glory of God. (Romans 3:23) This is original sin. It is inherent in the human race, passed on to each baby at conception, and dwells within the thoughts, imagination, and intents of the heart. God's Word, defined as the Lord Jesus Christ, is the discerner of such, and as with a two edged sword, divides man's spirit from his soul and body that all things may appear naked. Open to the eyes of Him with whom we have to do, He must continue His work in the believer. (Hebrews 4:12-16; Philippians 1:6, 2:12-13; John 1:1-4)

The Seed of Man's Destruction

It was Eve who was deceived, and transgressed the law, but it was Adam who defied God's authority. In Adam we died unto God. Since the fruit was toxic to the core, Adam's seed came under judgment. Mankind began to get sick, and eventually, death came upon all creatures' great and small. No one has died without some bodily organ becoming toxic. Sickness, even cancer and such, are more rampant now than ever before, but under the judgment of God, all die physically. Human beings are in the seed of Adam. We are born in the "likeness" of Adam, and separated from the image of God, sinners by the law of procreation. (Genesis 5:1-5) All creatures are in bondage and wait to be set free.

A Christian is one whose old creation (man) is crucified. (Galatians 2:20) Taken from Adam's natural likeness, God the Father destroys that old creation by placing it under judgment through Christ's death. When the new creation (new me) is raised in Christ, God's righteousness is implanted, and born without sin after Christ; the yoke of judgment is broken through our co-death, co-burial, and co-resurrection. Christ became sin for us so we might live as the righteousness of God in Christ Jesus. (2Corinthians 5:21) This is justification. (Hosea 6:1-3; Romans 4:25, 5:18) This is resurrection glory, wherein the creature (new me) waits for the liberty set for the children of God. (Romans 8:19-21)

This spiritual truth, if compared with a grandfather who died at the age of six, his grandchild would never be born. Naturally there are no grandchildren, because the family seed ended in the death of Grandfather. If the seed of Christ (in Abraham) is to be revived, then it must be sown in death, and manifest itself again in resurrection. (Romans 6:3-6; Galatians 3:13-18)

The Blemish

A person thinks nothing of exchanging a blemished, poor fitting garment for one that is clean, and fits properly. Usually the store proprietor is glad, especially if he wants to stay in business. Even so, when a person comes to God to exchange their life in Adam, God is pleased to oblige and to place (baptize) them in Christ. In exchange, the blemish brought through sin is annulled, and a new creature in Christ Jesus, does emerge. (2 Corinthians 5:17)

Further, when two agree on any one thing, and they ask the Father in agreement, shall it not happen? (Matthew 18:19-20) Just as a poor fitting garment draws criticism, an ungodly life draws criticism. God promises those who come to Him an abundant life, and in exchange, dresses and houses them appropriately. The blemished child may act out of old wounds, yet when revived and made new, are healed in resurrection. New life begins without shame and blame. (2 Peter 2:9-22)

The Healing

Revival affects the entire person, the body, soul, and spirit. Man is a three part being. One needs to know their body is not their soul, their soul is not their spirit, and their spirit is not their soul. Yet, all three are significant as man. The same applies to the tri-unity of God. The Father is not the Son, the Son is not the Spirit, and the Spirit is not the son. Yet, all three are manifest as God. The Word of God is consistent at its source. God made man a body from chemical elements in the earth, He breathed His Life into that body, and man became a living soul. (Genesis 2:7)

Revival affects the intellect (thinker), the emotions (feeler), and the will (chooser). These are psychological components of the soul, or personality. The effects of revival involve the Holy Spirit's entrance to the spirit of man. It gives rise to a conscience, an intuition, and a communicator of the Holy Spirit. (Romans 8:16; 1 Corinthians 3:16) Revival affects the body as boundaries set by physical characteristics. These affect man in relationship to God. The healing process of the Holy Spirit in the spirit transforms the soul or personality, and preserves the body for redemption. This too, will take place shortly. Current events keeps one focused in preparation for the Lord's return in the air. (1 Thessalonians 4:16-18; 2 Thessalonians 2:7) Then this mortal body will take on immortality. (1 Corinthians 15:53)

To reject the experience of new life in resurrection is a ploy of those who live after the flesh and in contradiction to their knowledge of God. (2 Corinthians 10:3-6) Some

Christians avoid revival because of the expressions associated with the term. Expressions such as the second blessing, a filling of the Spirit, a baptism of the Spirit, or a baptism of fire are relative. We associate revival with confession, surrender, submission, and subjective feelings that may or may not be true in experience. Even the words "born again" are taken out of context by reason of indifference. Seems everybody; everything, or everyplace can be subjected to some kind of new birth. New life in resurrection is simply a new "me" in Christ!

In the simplest form, revival takes place when the Holy Spirit of God brings the Christian, under the will of God, unto obedience. Perhaps one could think metaphorically. A Central Processing Unit (CPU) is likened to the Mind of Christ. (1 Corinthians 2:16) Prior to the installation of a CPU, one releases all data as the knowledge of God. All rights to corporate control are released. Corporately these are holy, acceptable, and ordained of God and given over to His service as a living sacrifice. (Romans 12:1-2) The effects surrounding the Christian's control centre are held sacred, and in the confidence of Christ.

Revival is a simple process. The enemy of the cross is the flesh. Nature affects self-esteem. It was the flesh that interpreted the claims of the serpent. If God did not mean they would die, then what influenced Eve to transgress the law by eating of the forbidden fruit? Selfish pride does not admit easily to being wrong. Pride is also what keeps one from entering into identification with Christ's death. The idea that we too, must surely die, is foreign to man's reason. It is in spiritual death, wherein the power of resurrection is employed. A Christian can access the joy of overcoming the law of sin to enter rest in the promised land. It has nothing to do with physical death. So, when self bows to the power of the Holy Spirit, God brings to the Believer a healing by restoring the promises of redemption preserved in Christ Jesus. (Ephesians 1:2-6)

A Band-Aid

A band-aid will cover a wound, and keep it clean, but healing takes place in the blood. "Be transformed by the renewing of the mind." The passage is a metamorphism. It means to change one's form. A butterfly is a disfigured worm. It must go through a stage of transition. Revival does not go through a stage of transition. Revival begets a new structure out of which the Christian lives. Some would compare reform with transform. Reform is the process of fitting into a different life style, but in the image and likeness of the reformist. Transform is exchanging the old image and likeness with the image of Christ in new life. This new image manifests all the attributes of Christ who is the first born to resurrection Life. Christian brethren naturally follow thereafter. (Romans 5:19, 8:29)

Individuals reason with a conceptual mind, rather than a contextual mind. The former process data over time and the role is played out in progression. The world identifies and labels the reality of that role, and expects an individual to live accordingly. A Christian attempts to justify their self-esteem. While doing in order to perform, the need to be is often overlooked. So, just how does one continue to fit within the family, group, and community? Something happened. Things no longer fit. Things are turned upside down, doubt, worry, and depression follow.

The latter mind will contextualize the new data into sets of cause and effect. The Believer remains clothed with an earthly suit yet prepared for the indwelling Spirit of God. The revived Christian maintains a life support system from a position of rest prepared for the people of God. (Hebrews 4:9-10) In Christ, they release the earthly control over to the indwelling Holy Spirit. Band-aids are not for healing, they are a covering, and cannot hold together the structure of a new life in Christ. The human mind associates with things of the world, and depend on reason, but the mind of Christ is set apart unto God.

The Template

History, observed and understood through a pattern of events, displays a person's character. Every human being has a template or genetic code called D.N.A. The template determines how a person will develop, and grow in the ageing process. History is already in place. There is a migratory system built within many species of living organisms that directs its destiny. A Believer, upon confession of faith is accepted in the Beloved, destined for resurrection, and the characteristics of the new life in Christ are set. (Ephesians 1:6) Acceptance comes complete with a new pattern, a new template, a new spiritual code (DNA) for development and maturation.

A new structure replaces old ideas with new ideas. A new processing format is put in place by the Holy Spirit. A struggle for control over the new life becomes more ferocious than ever, especially if one has grown up in a religious life style. Unless, these biased thoughts come under the control of New Structure, there is no peace.

Until self-bows to the Son of God, the Holy Spirit cannot reveal the will of God, but if in a state of readiness, can be set free from the bondage sin. (1 Timothy 1:7)

Retained with memories of past sin, the imagination becomes a stronghold and keeps the soul in bondage. It is well programmed with associations and things of the past, and is a stronghold for divisive spirits. These are brought under the influence of the Word of God. Thoughts and intents of the heart are brought into captivity and subjected to the obedience of Christ. When these are captured, and taken in obedience, the power of resurrection is activated. (2 Corinthians 10:6)

Anger is a thought supported by reason, and is a short-range goal that seeks to avenge any threat to religious morality. In every situation, the Christian's response is to exchange denominational biased thoughts with the attributes of new life in Christ. A Christian's response, when threatened with bias, seeks to control the personality. The psychological defenses of the mind, war against the Spirit over the control of the new creature in Christ. (2 Corinthians 10:6; Galatians 5:17)

Life in the resurrection delivers the believer from resentful and obsessive thoughts. Opening the gateway to the soul for spiritual intercession, new thoughts will be delivered from the Holy Spirit, and confirmed by the Word of God. Feelings, kindled with thoughts not to be trusted, tend to change with the times. Like a fire burning out of control, circumstance, trauma, and physical stress, will cause varying degrees of strain. The gateway between the soul and spirit is blocked by this burning inferno fueled by recessed and hostile thoughts. Life in the resurrection is an extinguishing agent giving access to the Holy Spirit, delivering the believer from vain imagination, fantasy, paranoia, and schizophrenia that embitter the soul. The template, upon which the former was infatuated, must be broken. God, in His infinite wisdom, desires the believer to repent and be cured of the disease caused by sin.

The Cure

Repentance is the key to cure. The Christian is in Christ, yet, hindered while living in the shadow of revenge filled with bitterness, strife, competition, and hatred. Confused and frightened thoughts disappear as times of refreshing come from being in the presence of the Lord. (Acts 3:19) Believers must learn to appropriate daily by denying self, and learn to bring thoughts captive unto the Lord Jesus in obedience. Expect old patterns of living to be replaced with brand new patterns for living out the abundant Life. Experience life in the Resurrection, and when He returns in Glory, you return as His Glory. (Philippians 3:10; Colossians 3:4)

Believers are crucified with Christ. (Galatians 2:20) The old "me" is placed into His death. The old "me" is buried in Christ. A new "me" is raised free from sin. (Ephesians 2:5-6) Therefore, my brothers and sisters in the Lord, we are dead to the law by the body of Christ. Now, being married to another, even to Him who is raised from the dead, we are to bring forth fruit unto God. (Romans 7:1-4) His Grace justifies us through the redemption that is in Christ Jesus. (Romans 3:24; Ephesians 2:6) That is the preface to revival.

Throughout this chapter new life was identified as revival. The term revival was never meant to be an event happening outside the body. To live again was prefaced as being raised from the dead as a new creature. The old nature was discarded as flesh. In order to live again, something or some one had to die. In this case, it was the old man, the self, or the humanity of man. The nature of man, based in Adam, was crucified, and a new creature was created in exchange for the old. The new "me" is in Christ. This new "me" is further explained in the next chapter, "A New Identity in Christ."

CHAPTER THREE

A NEW IDENTITY IN CHRIST

The Window of Death

There is a story told by G. W. Target entitled, "The Window," which tells of two men, both seriously ill, who occupied the same small hospital room. One man was allowed to sit up in his bed for an hour each afternoon to drain the fluid from his lungs. His bed was next to the room's only window. The other man had to spend all his time flat on his back.

The men talked for hours on end. They spoke of their wives and families, their homes, their jobs, their involvement in the military service, and where they spent their vacations. Every afternoon, when the man in the bed by the window could sit up, he would pass the time by describing to his roommate all the things he could see outside his window. The man in the other bed began to live for those one-hour periods where his world would be broadened and enlivened by all the activity and color of the outside world.

The window overlooked a park with a lovely lake, the man said ducks and swans played on the water while children sailed their model boats. Lovers walked arm in arm amidst flowers of every color of the rainbow. Grand old trees graced the landscape, and a fine view of the city skyline could be seen in the distance. As the man by the window described all this in such vivid detail, the man on the other side of the room would close his eyes and imagine the picturesque scene. One warm afternoon the man by the window described a parade passing. Although the other man could not hear the band, he could see it in his mind's eye as the gentleman by the window portrayed it with such descriptive words. Suddenly, an alien thought came into his head: Why should he have all the pleasure of seeing everything while I never get to see anything? It did not seem to be fair.

As the thought soured in his mind he felt ashamed at first, but as the days passed and he missed out on seeing more sights, his envy eroded into resentment and soon turned him into a bitter old man. He began to brood and he found himself unable to sleep. He should be by that window; that obsessive thought controlled his life.

Late one night as he was staring at the ceiling, the man by the window began to cough. He was choking on the fluid in his lungs. The other man watched in the dimly lit room as the struggling man by the window groped for the button to call for help. Listening from across the room, he never moved, never pushed his button, which would have brought the nurse running. In less than five minutes the coughing and choking stopped, along with the sound of breathing. Now there was only silence, a deathly silence.

The following morning the day nurse arrived to bring water for their baths. When she found the lifeless body of the man by the window, she was saddened and called the hospital attendants to take it away, no words, no fuss, just take it away. As soon as it seemed appropriate, the other man asked if he might be moved close to the window. The nurse was happy to make the switch, and after making sure he was comfortable, she left him alone.

Slowly, painfully he propped himself up on one elbow to take his first look. Finally, he would have all the joy of seeing it for himself. He strained as he looked out the window beside his bed. It faced a blank wall. (Swindoll, 1992)

Resurrected Life after Death identifies who we are in Christ. No one comes to the Father except in Christ Jesus. The new "me" is in Christ, in heaven, now! It is certain that circumstances and belief systems are not the things that provide the Christian lasting joy, let alone peace of mind and the Abundant Life. Crossing over Jordan, to many believers, is physical death. In this book, crossing over Jordan is identification with Christ in His death, burial, resurrection, and ascension. The greatest hindrance to accepting this truth is a reasoning mind. It contributes to a religious bias that continual confession of forgiven sin is necessary to salvation. Confession calls for repentance wherein all unrighteousness is forgiven. (1 John 1:9; 4:15)

A Bag of Beliefs

The Protestant Church is a mixture of a biased belief system. Soon, the Christ of the Gospels will no longer even be a prerequisite to salvation. (U.S. News, 2008)

The Moderator of the United Church of Canada recently denied belief in the Divinity of Christ. (Canadian News, 1997) Does the same belief system apply to the ministers and congregation of the United Church? See footnote on a more recent report. (U.S. News, 2008) Where can the sheep of these pastures look for help?

The doctrine of salvation is the foundational teaching of Christianity. It is the cornerstone of the Christian belief. It is used to differentiate between Christianity and other religions. Now, all hope is lost. The Christmas story is no longer the story of the Divine Birth, but an analogy of a story from history. The Easter bunny has become a resurrected chicken. Christianity is a travesty of beliefs.

The Path of Division

The Protestant Movement began with Justification by Faith as posited by Martin Luther. (1483-1546) It showed the need for saving faith outside the sacraments of the Ordained Church. Election by Grace, later established through the teachings of John Calvin (1509-1564), showed the need for a Sovereign God. It was modified by James Arminius (1560-1609), as Election of Progressive Grace, and showed God as being less demanding. History shows how Christian uniformity gave way to religious diversity, and by 1648, an individual could read and interpret the Word of God without fear. (Cairns, 1967) The wedge of indifference was set in tablets of stone.

A diversity of belief systems nullifies the affect of persecution. Any Christian who desires to live a Godly life in Christ shall suffer persecution. (2 Timothy 3:12)

There is too much diversity within the Christian faith, and denominationalism has become a host to bias. Theologians have weighed the pros and cons of the Christian faith for centuries, and have yet to tip the scales in any one positive direction. The directive is to be tolerant one with the other, patient and long-suffering, keeping the tone of tolerance among people of religious diversity, and walk on different paths. Who dares stand in the solidarity of faith alone?

The Illusion

Persecution is the standard for those called to live Godly in Christ Jesus. Where thought soured the Christian mind, shame has failed, and blame has turned to envy. The two men in the hospital story gave the illusion that a biased view from a window is not always the way it is intended.

Christians miss out on the pleasures of the world. Alien thoughts erode into resentment and turn one into bitter old men. Christians, who dwell on circumstances of life, soon find themselves unable to cope with pressures of life. Pastors have breakdowns. Sunday is gone by the way, and prophets leave Biblical research to facilitate teaching from denominational manuals.

A resentful thought is a controller of Christian life. It is similar to that picturesque scene portrayed from the window; an illusion of a biased mind and masks the truth of the Gospel of Christ. Those, who listen to imaginative thoughts, miss out on the reality of a Godly life. They sit undecided watching as leaders weigh the pros and cons through endless rhetoric. Personal bias creates an illusive zeal and blocks the Way of the Cross.

The Noise

There is a mural, located in the old Supreme Court Building, Lausanne, Switzerland, painted by Paul Robert (1851-1923) that he entitled Justice Lifts the Nations (1905). He painted the title on the mural itself so the meaning would remain clear. The mural has "Justice" standing without blindfold, and pointing with her sword toward the Law of God. The Bible is the authority by which the law unfolds. The scales of Justice is of no mere consequence, but one of exquisite meaning to the ideals of the Protestant Reformation. (Schaeffer, 1976)

In trying to understand the idealism and diversity of the contemporary Christian Church, consider a television set where two or more channels can be viewed simultaneously. The main channel is assertive while other channels deliver a lesser message. (Miller, 1978) The viewer has the option of choice. There is little or no interaction. Structure, process, function, interaction and interrelationships intercept the pattern; a decision is made on the basis of experience. Christians, who attempt to reason over two or more interpretive passages, have a problem. Who can watch the News on channel seven, and Sex in the City on channel four, without having a problem? The truth is, the second channel is delivering its message with significant loss to the content of the first channel. As an example in Japan, a Children's daytime show had the eyes of its main character flash incessantly. This caused children to suffer epileptic fits. (National News, 1997) The endless noise of rhetoric creates problems in discerning the factual interpretation of truth.

There are many Bibles, religions, and ideologies. How does the Christian make sense of any message? How can they untangle all this biased noise? The Japanese Children's program is but one example, but what about the people next door, down the street, or across town, they too, may be controlled by some insidious ploy of mind play. Amidst the noise of rhetoric, is it any wonder the discerning Christian is unable to connect between what to believe, and whom to believe.

St. Paul, in his address to the Athenian's Unknown God, put it this way; "And He has made from One, every Nation of people to dwell on all the face of the earth, and has pre-appointed times and boundaries of their dwellings, so that they should seek the Lord, in the hope they might find Him through groping, though He is not far from each of us." It was not until Paul mentioned the reality of the "resurrection" that they began to mock and so asked him to come back another time. (Acts 17:26-27, 32) Jesus, in the raising of Lazarus said, "I am the resurrection and the life." (John 11:25) There is One who can deliver, He is Lord. Diversity, if fine-tuned can hear the message of the gospel. There is only one Lord, one Faith, and one Baptism. (Ephesians 4:4-6)

God's Sacrifice

The word grope means to feel about as in the dark, to move about in an awkward incoherent manner, showing a need to know and understand, but swayed by reason, and fed by emotion. Jesus Christ is not revealed through the emotion, mind, or will, but through the Spirit. He is a historical person. Emotions cannot relate to the Person of Christ except as they flow between the soul and spirit. (Miller, 1978)

The work of the Spirit is one work, but the works of the flesh are many. Christians relate to the world. They tend to philosophize than use the Word of God to substantiate truth. Truth can only be substantiated through the Word of God. It must be held absolute in matters of spiritual faith and practice. No phenomenon of experience should be mixed with the truth of God's Word, nor should feelings be allowed to interfere with interpretation. The answer to the problem of diversity within the Christian Church is not if it feels good, but can it be substantiated with the Word of God?

Christianity is not a feel good religion. It is a relationship with Jesus, the Son of God. He came to give His life as a blood sacrifice. God must condemn wicked men. On that tree He bore our sin and He became sin, bearing our guilt, he became a curse. Christ redeemed us from the curse becoming a curse in our place. If God is just, His judgment must be carried out to the letter. Because there was no other sacrifice, Abraham lifted his blade to kill his only son Jacob. He was stopped, and given a ram. Even so, God saw fit to kill His only begotten son. There was no other sacrifice. (Genesis 22:9-13; Ephesians 5:2; Hebrews 10:12)

The Gospel

Every person within earshot of the Gospel of Christ has heard the good news of salvation, but many choose not to listen. If they believed the Scriptures, out of which Jesus of Nazareth claimed to be the Way, the Truth, and the Life, the confessional would be empty. (John 14:6) Jesus said of Himself, "Believe that I am in the Father, and the Father is in me: or else believe me for the sake of the work. You know, and I'll say this one more time, He that believes on me, the work that I do shall he do also; even more work than this because I'm going home to the Father. Whatsoever you ask in my name I'll do, so the Father may be glorified in the Son." (John 14:10-14) This is relationship.

Jesus, after He was raised from the dead and seen over a period of forty days, went back home to the Father in heaven. He is seated at the Father's right hand. Most denominations teach Jesus as being raised physically from the dead by the power of the Father, but some teach He only rose in the Spirit. Christianity is the only religion that teaches that a child born of a virgin would be the Savior, who is Christ the Lord. (Luke 2:11) The Child Jesus grew as any other child into an adult and as all men, would die. What makes the death of this man Jesus different from other men?

Jesus not only told of how He would die, but that He would be raised from the dead physically in a matter of three days. His Divinity was not altered by His death on the cross. It was His body that suffered the shame of transgression. It is through His flesh that the Christian enters the new and living way, boldly entering the Holiest through His blood. (Hebrews 10:19-20) The Christian is crucified with Christ, placed into His death, buried, and raised again to new life. (Romans 6:3-6) Is this so hard to understand? Is it so foolish? It can only be understood through faith. Life in the power of the resurrection is a faith belief system.

Structure of Resurrection

Jesus, as a man, showed Himself to His disciples as having an identifiable personality. Thomas touched His new resurrected body. After which, Jesus gave Thomas peace in understanding the structure of resurrection. Jesus entered the room without opening a door. The structure of His resurrected body gave access through the walls of a room. (John 20:26-29) Jesus is the first to receive such a body raised from the dead, but not the last. (1 Corinthians 15:50-53) The law of revived sin and death was challenged and defeated by Jesus on the Cross. The Christian, is placed into His body of death, buried, and raised together in His resurrection. The Christian is at rest waiting for the redemption of the body. (Ephesians 1:13) Until then, they are in Christ Jesus, at the right hand of the Father. (Romans 6:3-6; Galatians 2:20; Ephesians 2:5-6, 22)

The old man is crucified and buried. The new man, (Christian) is alive in the resurrected Christ in heaven. On earth, he no longer has the corrupted nature of the first Adam, but the divine nature of the second Adam, Christ Jesus. (2 Peter 1:1-4) This nature is incorruptible and without sin conceived as the very Word of God, who lives and abides forever. He gave His life that we might abide with Him in heaven. Our window does not open to a brick wall, but it opens to a new identity in Christ. Resurrected life after death is a walk of victory.

This chapter sought to identify the Christian as being in Christ. The death of Christ assured the believer of a place in resurrection. The Believer is placed into Christ's death, buried with Him in the tomb, and then raised with Him in Glory. Many would believe it was just a spirit, but His resurrected body must have substance, and contain within the fruit of His loins, the new me. "Therefore if any man be in Christ, he is a new creature: old things are passed away; behold all things are become new." (2 Cor. 5:17) This, to the reasoning mind, may be hard to understand. The next Chapter, "Apathy within The Clergy" will show how the clergy paints this creature as being positional, or in the state of being arranged, or as provisional *status quo*.

Chapter Four

Apathy Within the Clergy

A Cry in the Wilderness

Few church members take their religion seriously. Believers who are born again in Christ, all too soon experience frustration over the apathy shown by their pastors. How does theology influence Christianity?

Setting biblical truth before clergy is intimidating. The theology mind-set of most pastors is closed except to a denominational point of view. Theology has imposed countless biased beliefs on the Christian. Ever since the resurrection, men have tried to persuade through rhetoric. When one begins to take the Christian faith seriously, church leadership is often in opposition.

Pastors put the organizational needs of the church first. This leaves the parishioners to find their way alone. Some do teach the Gospel, but only from the theology position of their denomination. Even when they disagree, they dare not express such disagreement for fear of losing their position. Artemus Ward made this remark, "It ain't so much the things we don't know that gets us in trouble, but the things that we know that ain't so." (Class notes, Oxford Graduate School, 1992)

Those who support Calvinism, Arminianism, Catholicism, Christian Science, and many more, have a theological mind-set. Most never question the source of doctrine. They do not know they do not know, and never confront theological heresy. Paul the Apostle, in Acts Chapter seventeen verse twenty-eight said, "for in Him we all live and move and have our being, . . . For we are His offspring."

Is this not evidence for the fruit of His loins? What did Paul mean by these words? Can you identify body, soul, and spirit the tri-unity of man from this passage? Hidden in context we find that: In Him we live (spirit), in Him we move (body), in Him we have our being (soul). Theologically speaking, we are three persons in one corporate body, a tri-partite individual. (Acts 17:24-30; Hebrews 4:12) Some say the soul and the spirit are the same entity, that the old nature and new nature are nested; those who teach such have a biased theology.

The text, from Paul's message to the Athenians at Mars Hill, concluded with supporting structure from poetry that spoke of God being their God. Paul's denunciation is that they were attempting to worship God as some creation such as gold, silver, and stone. The message is mere philosophy. God overlooks some degree of ignorance, but commands all people everywhere to repent, turn away, and deny images set before that distort the will of God.

How many Christians stop and think about what they really believe? Can they support their belief system with Scripture? Most Christians cannot explain biblically what they believe, yet are quick to support how they feel. Take a close look over the last few years, months, days, and even hours of your life. Does your belief system support what you know "to be" true, or only what you have been told? How do you feel? Perhaps you do not know, or you know, but are unsure of what you know.

The Word of God

In the days before the printing press, few had access to the written Word. In these last days, God has given modern society the ability to transliterate and understand different languages. It is important that this modern day technology not be taken for granted. It has not evolved to cause a new culture of super beings. The Bible was translated from Hebrew, Greek, and Aramaic into every language in the modern world, so mankind may know God, and His Son Jesus is not perceived in nature, the psyche, or some meta-physical aberration. The written Word is to be perceived as The Living Word of God. (John 1:1; Hebrews 1:1; Revelation 1:1)

The need to have the Bible in print was the motivation that led to the design of the printing press. It was in 1456 when Johannes Gutenberg printed his famous 42-line Bible. Each column had 42 lines of print. Many Christians were told by their pastors the art of printing was some devious form of "black" art that came from Satan. Now that must be some biased teaching?

In North America, an Italian printer, Juan Pablos, set up a print shop in Mexico City in 1539. One hundred years later in 1639 the American colonies got their first print shop. It was in Cambridge, Mass, under the direction of Stephen Day and his son Matthew. Since then, a massive population explosion has taken place.

All have the opportunity of hearing and reading. Except for some third world countries, the good news that God loves them, sent His only begotten Son Jesus to live on earth some thirty three years, died for the curse of mankind, and after three days raised from the dead. This action set us free from the bondage of Adam's sin. The Word of God, printed in every man's language, is available to every person who wants to know the way of eternal life.

There were no print shops in Paul's day. The gift of speaking in various languages (tongues) was an absolute necessity to proclaim the Gospel to people from other nations. Many spoke with different dialects and languages, but God made it clear through language uttered under the direction of the Holy Spirit. Books, articles, and tracts are now written and published that express and emphasize the Gospel of Christ. Any tongue that cannot be interpreted should not be spoken. However, there is no excuse not to read the Bible.

Research data show that some read their Bible longer and more often because there are translations written without old English phraseology. Many thee's and thou's of the King James Bible, are removed, and modern syntax and spelling put in place. It remains that the Holy Spirit must reveal God's Word to the believer. Each book is addressed to certain people, a nation, or person, and that includes you and me. (Ephesians 1:1) Where is the original Bible?

Modern Theology is appealing to many Christians. It can be traced from the importation of German idealistic philosophy early in the nineteenth century. Biblical criticism was transferred from Scottish and German Seminaries where American Bible students went to study theology, amidst the teaching of evolution formulated by Charles Darwin. (Cairns, 1967)

Many have studied in Alexandria, Egypt, where Hebrew, Aramaic, and Greek words of the Bible have been broken apart and replaced with modern day thought and syntax. These Bible students turned theologians, are literary and language experts. These aspiring students of God's Word study these translations and versions of the Holy Scriptures with the intent to clarify, but often confuse.

Alexandria of Egypt vs Antioch of Syria

Many of the original letters of Paul were penned in Antioch, in ancient Syria now southern Turkey. In the second century, a disciple by the name of Lucian founded a school of Scriptures in Antioch. His school magnified the authority and divinity of Scripture, and taught that the Bible was to be taken literally. Antioch accepted the Bible to be literally God's words. God's promise assures us that the Words of the Lord are pure words. God keeps His Word and preserves them from generation to generation and forever. (Psalm 12:6-7) Can anyone dispute God's Word?

Solomon, the wisest man who ever lived, ignored God's Biblical admonition to avoid Egypt. (Deuteronomy 17:16-17) However, he wanted to increase his drove of horses.

So, he went down to Egypt. He not only brought back multiple horses, but he also brought back multiple wives. (1 Kings 3:1; 10:28) The result, his heart was turned away from following God, and he began worshipping other gods. God pronounced judgment on him. (1 Kings 11:3-43) Has the mind of God changed over the years? If God did not want Solomon to go down to Egypt for horses, what is the risk of theologians going to Egypt to study and translate the Bible?

"The words of the LORD are pure words: as silver tried in a furnace of earth, purified seven times. Thou shalt keep them, O LORD, thou shalt preserve them from this generation for ever." (Psalms 12:6-7) It is not just the way letters, words, sentences, paragraphs, or diagrams, are drawn and written, but too, they must be spiritually illuminating. It is a Living Word, and must be understood with spiritual insight. Adding and changing prepositions, verses, and text to the Holy Bible cause great confusion. It is God who is owner and source of His Holy Word. Through reading His Word, and trusting the Holy Spirit to lead, the Christian will grow and mature in Grace.

The Messenger of Grace

God gave Paul revelation to establish a ministry to the Gentiles. A Gentile is one not of the commonwealth of Israel. Paul received a thorn in his flesh that he may not think of himself a measure above God's Grace. This thorn was a physical object used by the messenger of Satan to keep Paul aware of his ministry. He was obliged to yield to the leading of the Holy Spirit. Any self-directed confidence would be redirected, and committed to the sufficiency of God's Grace. (2 Corinthians 12:7-10)

Paul knew the Old Testament inside out with the laws and sacraments. Paul, who was then Saul, was a disclaimer to the experience of the Way. It was not until the resurrected Jesus stopped him on the Damascus road that he realized the error of his way. He wrote most of the New Testament as he participated and observed the behaviors of those who gave credence, and experienced Power in Resurrection. The Acts of the Apostles were written on parchment, carried in packsacks, and printed in every language. This is not coincidental.

The Holy Bible is available for all to read, to experience, and to teach, and proclaim the Gospel of Jesus Christ. The Word of God in the Holy Bible is complete. There are no extra biblical utterances that can claim to be God's Word. The Christian is complete in Christ. There is no more work, séances, or meta-physical signs or wonders. Jesus, our Lord and Savior, is the Head of all principality and power. It is He who purchased us by His blood, and in captivity, makes us to sit with Him in heavenly places.

The Christian, being placed into Christ's death, resurrected and ascended in Christ, is an experiential reality. The body is yet to be redeemed. It is preserved for redemption, and with the trumpet call of God, it will be caught up to the clouds of the air as immortal and incorruptible. (1 Corinthians 15:52-57; 1 Thessalonians 4:14-17) The Christian, in crucifying the old man, has buried the old nature, and is raised a new creature in Christ. All this is accomplished through the faith and operation of God. (Romans 6:3-6; Ephesians 2:6; Colossians 2:10-12)

The Lies

From time to time revival does happen. Do not believe for a moment that the Christian, who has identified with new Life in Christ, is on cloud nine twenty-four-seven. Life hurts when a Christian learns that what their Church believes cannot be supported through Biblical context. Pastors, with a mixture of feelings, pride, and bias, often coerce new Christians into accepting false theological.

The Christ gave up His status as God, became flesh, and in humility, dwelt among us as man. Yet, He was given for our salvation. It is a spiritual let down to believe in an all-powerful God, and then be told Jesus Christ is not the only Way to eternal Life. (U.S. News, 2008) This is false theological. It brings doubt to the mind of the Christian. We must search diligently the Scripture, for in searching the Word of God, one is led to trust and believe the Word of God. (John 5:17-39; Ephesians 1:13)

The Holy Spirit reveals God's will to the Christian. While many doctrines are supplemented with psychological jargon, and so-called extra-biblical revelation, a believer who experiences new life in resurrection, often becomes depressed over the cover-up of truth. God alone can show mercy and compassion. There is no need for continual confession. Self is difficult to deny, and death is absolute.

There is nothing more distressful than to find one fail in the practice of biblical doctrine. It may be the Pastor, a Sunday School Teacher, or other Church worker who is caught up with literature that undermines the integrity of the Word of God, the Deity of Christ, and is lead down the road to trust in self help books. It is as if God can only be trusted when it feels good.

The Jealousy of God

The Spirit that indwells the Christian is a jealous Spirit. The law is clear. One shall not covet another's possession. It is against the law. To take by force, to interrogate, or to coerce another is wrong. Cain coveted Abel's offering to the Lord. Each was presented to God, but God accepted Abel's offering and rejected Cain. Was it the person of Cain who was rejected, or was it his offering? God never rejects the person, but he does reject their offerings. In particular, God is not pleased with an offering deemed for greater acceptance. (Hebrews 10:5-10)

Cain had the opportunity to repent and make his offering acceptable, but he brooded over Abel's acceptance, and became bitter. Alas, when performance is above person, all too often both the person and the offering are rejected. Let the story show how Cain later killed his brother Abel. This is the first murder in the history of man that mediates the principle of covetousness and envy.

It took place long before the law was even written on tablets of stone. (Genesis 4:8) Do you see how sin can be revived, to live again, each time the Christian covets, each time one is envious of another person's possession, sin is revived. One should never look upon another in the way of covetousness, to envy, for greed leads to sin. How is it that so many Christians, entrenched with envy, jealousy and greed, cause division within the Church Family? (1

Corinthians 3:1-3) The Spirit moves to jealousy when one seeks acceptance through performance based works. This is the way of the world, not the way of the Cross.

Complaining is not part of the divine nature. Shall the Christian grieve the Holy Spirit to jealousy and test the Living God? With God, there is neither evil nor good, but righteousness. Wherefore does one complain? The Christian can attempt it their way, but the option of turning again in repentance unto the Lord, is always at the door. Be thankful, God is ever merciful to the Christian.

The Christian is sealed unto the day of redemption. Put all performance away. Anything that will grieve, or cause the Spirit to be jealous, put away. Bitterness, anger, bedlam, evil speaking one of another, back stabbing, resentment, let the Christian forgive the brother or sister in the Lord even as God for Christ's sake has forgiven, and cleansed from all unrighteousness. (Ephesians 4:30-32; 1 John 1:9) Life in resurrection, extinguishes complaints by which the Divine Nature of Christ permeates the life. (2 Peter 1:4)

God sent His Spirit of Comfort in which to bathe. What about being so filled with self, that another, who is hurting is left without care? The Spirit has every reason to be jealous of flirtations with the world and jealous over flirtations with self. The Christian should not be so caught up with self-help books, exercise routines, and nutritional remedies, as to set themselves apart from the world.

The Father of our Lord Jesus Christ is the God of comfort. He comforts the Christian that one may know how to comfort another, including the ungodly, the washed and the unwashed. He does not say how, when, or where to comfort, He simple says to be a comfort.

The Anger of God

Is an eye for an eye and a tooth for a tooth politically correct in the twenty first century? Jesus said, "The child of God is not to resist evil: but whoever would strike one on the right cheek, turn to him the left. Should one take your coat, give him your shirt. Go the extra mile, and should one ask to borrow, never refuse." Jesus says, "Love the enemy, bless those who curse you, and don't reject those who would reject. Why? Because the Father in heaven causes the sun to shine on both the just and the unjust." (Matthew 5:38-48) This implies that God loves the sinner and the saint. He sheds light on those who sincerely look to His Church, His Body, for deliverance and healing. No person or group of persons has a monopoly on God's grace. Vengeance is mine, so says the Lord. Do not be disheartened if the Lord should choose to chastise a child He loves. (Romans 12:19; Hebrews 12:8)

Though the Christian may at times seem uncomforted, this is not an excuse not to be a comfort to another. (2 Corinthians 1:3-4)The Holy Spirit is the Christian's comforter. Through the Christian, the Holy Spirit will bring comfort to another, and by God's Grace and Mercy, reconcile them unto Himself. The Christian is trying to do the comfort thing, trying to do the encouraging thing, but neglects the simple command; to be a comfort. The Spirit does not give a "to do" model, but a "to be" model.

Therefore, be a comfort. He comforts those who would come to Him in faith, and without fear of rejection.

The Acceptance of God

Rejection is the absence of meaningful love. Learning how to perform love and how to perform comfort is counter-productive to love. Love of resurrection glory kindles the flames of freedom. The fruit of the Spirit is love, joy, peace, patience, kindness, goodness, faith, generosity, sobriety, and self-restraint. Against such, there is no law, no fear of rejection. Love is the standard. (Galatians 5:22-23) All too many Christians are taught they must perform. This is conditional. The presence of meaningful love gives meaning and acceptance to the heart of God.

Christian is loved without condition. A Christian should never be judged by what they do, but for who they are in Christ. Individuals should be accepted on who they are, not by what they are, or how well endowed with talents and abilities to perform. Performance based Christians need love without conditions.

There is a difference between individual and individualism. The individual is a person with a unique persona that fits within the structure of the whole. Most have experienced loving relationships, and some not so loving. These relationships should, by identification, show the absurdity of acceptance through performance. A sign with the message, "No conditions necessary" should be written on every Church door. Nothing should stand between the searching soul, and a loving God!

One reason the Church is not teaching life in resurrection is expectation. What does a Christian do as a member of a denominational Church that would not be accepted in a Church that is sharing new life in resurrection? Christians who are psyched up in role-playing are not prepared to lay down their life as Christ did for the Church. Christ loved the Church and gave Himself for it; That He might present to Himself a glorious Church, not having spot, or blame, or any such thing, but that it should be holy and without blemish, sanctified and cleansed with the refreshing, invigorating water of the Word. (Ephesians 5:1-33)

There is no greater commandment than to love your neighbor as yourself. Who is your neighbor? It is the person sitting in the back pew, in the hospital, or at home alone. It is the man or woman, the boy or girl down the street, the family that just experienced the loss of a job or loved one. These need the comfort of the Holy Spirit. One who lives in resurrection can uphold the Pastor in ministry. The laity is to know Christ, the Power of resurrection, His fellowship in suffering, leading others to denial of self. (Luke 9:23; Philippians 3:8-15)

Theology of sin is in control. Ever since the resurrection, men have tried to persuade by rhetoric. It is time to practice the Word of God. Many pastors seem to have forgotten how to pastor, how to visit the sick, how to counsel the bereaved, and most, either do not know, care, or take the time to edify the believer. A Christian young, old, carnal, or mature, are in Christ, in resurrection. The call is to the pastor and to the church, and to Christian awakening. Revival is in the making, and the message for the pastor, and to the world is, "make ready for behold He comes with ten thousands of His Saints, so make straight the path of His Way. (Jude 1:24) The world is in an economic crisis. Jesus is coming soon!

This chapter captured the ideology of many pastors. State run churches are not the same as congregational run churches, yet pastors are mostly all the same. All too often they seek to obey the doctrines of the church rather than the doctrines of the Bible. The congregation needs sound theological teaching. It is the prayer of this author that the following chapter, "The Foundation of Genesis" will encourage and develop a better understanding of just how badly "sin" is misunderstood among Christians.

CHAPTER FIVE

THE FOUNDATION OF GENESIS

The Reason

The creation account provides historical evidence for Genesis. The beginning of man's sojourn on planet earth tells all. The first eleven chapters of Genesis lay the foundation for all living systems, including mankind. If these chapters were factually interpreted, the meaning for life and death, good and evil, sin and righteousness, love and hate, could be better understood.

Substance abuse is better understood in light of Adam as falling from grace. Substance is the cause and effect of sin. Alcohol is a chemical that can be identified in all fruit. It is implied the fruit of the tree of the knowledge of good and evil contained ethanol. Could this substance affect the thinking process of Adam and Eve bring shame and blame to the community? (It is understood by the Hebrew that wine is to be mixed as two parts water and one part alcohol. The one part, ethanol, was not to be drank alone. Thus we have the fruit of the tree as one part, and the fruit of the vine as two parts.) Under the influence of the serpent, they acted contrarily to what they knew to be true of the Word of God. They anticipated judgment.

Noah found grace in the eyes of the Lord. After the great flood, Noah planted a vineyard, and drank the wine. His younger son Ham, found him drunk and naked. Ham was cursed by his father to be forever a servant to his brethren. (Genesis 9:20-25) Canaan, the son of Ham and father of the Canaanites, became the Nation of Palestine. Lying between the Jordan River and the Mediterranean Sea, this land was promised to Israel by God, and gave them the right to occupy. The present conflict is not a recent phenomenon.

Some define justification as, just as if it never happened; or total denial of blame. The sin of Adam passed upon all humanity. This sin of iniquity began in Adam, and was applicable to Noah, and all his sons who are the progeny ancestors of all men everywhere. The age of reason began with the denial of God's authority. Denial is an attribute centered on a conspiracy of unrighteousness. Reinforced by some inherent content ingested from the fruit taken off the tree of the knowledge of good and evil, denial set the stage for judgment. A common effect in the demise of good character in all humanity is the element of alcohol.

The Chemical

The environment of planet earth allowed humans to live nine hundred and sixty nine years. The man called Noah, walked with God six hundred years. This generation was corrupt and violent before God. He had no other choice than to destroy this generation. They became offensive in their thoughts, walked after an imagination perverted by evil, and looked upon Noah as foolish for building a boat when there was yet no rain upon the earth. God grieved over His creation. He would no longer tolerate humanity's abuse of this generation. (Genesis 6:13)

God decided to end this generation from the face of planet earth. He chose Noah, his three sons and their wives, with two of each kind of living creatures required to replenish the earth. God instructed Noah to build an ark to preserve them from a flood of waters that would come from within and without planet earth. Noah became a farmer after the flood, lived another three hundred and fifty years, and died. God limited subsequent generations of man to one hundred and ten years. (Genesis 6:1-9) As expressed in a Psalm of David, because of secret sins, we spend our years as a story told in years of threescore and ten, (70) and if by reason of strength they be fourscore, (80) yet in that strength we labor and sorrow. It is soon cut off, and we fly away. (Psalms 90:8-10) What a neat way of defining our golden years on planet earth.

Noah planted a vineyard, and became drunk on the wine. The judgment of sin came upon man and the environment. The washing of water does not destroy ethanol. A product of carbohydrate, alcohol and a wide variety of bacteria, fungi plants, and other life form are natural products of the earth, and are under the judgment of God.

Alcohol is everywhere organisms live. Products, of a Pharmaceutical nature, are used as medication to reduce some effects of the curse. They are classified by the chemical properties, mode of administration, and biological system. The system is referred to as the Anatomical Therapeutic Chemical Classification System (ATC system). (Reference.com) There is no fountain of youth.

The flood of waters did not destroy the reproductive seed of organisms, but only those who depended on breathing oxygen for life. (Genesis 6:17; 7:15, 22) Lying within the murky parts of marsh water, chemists isolate 0-2 mg/kg of alcohol. Garden soils contain 6 mg/kg, and flowers, beautiful as they may be, contain 16 mg/kg of alcohol. Shrubs producing red currents have 17- 41 mg/kg of alcohol. Ordinary fruits like an orange contain a whopping 473-552 mg/kg of alcohol, and the arctic bramble bush as much as 1200-1490 mg/kg of alcohol. (Forsander, 1998) Alcohol is a transparent inclusion innate in crystals. Composed of molecules and atoms, they are the first building block of living systems, the cell. (Miller, 1978)

.

The human body is made to process environmental chemicals. Alcohol in the body is oxidized by the liver at the rate of 7-8 grams per hour, and if in excess, monopolize 60 to 100 percent of the liver's capacity for producing parts suitable for extrusion from the body. Elements of alcohol compromise the function of neuronal membranes in the Central Nervous System. (Miller, 1978) Alcohol changes the calcium levels of the membranes and adjusts the tolerance and dependence levels in degrees in the suffering alcoholic. (Wadstein and Ohlin, n/d)

Yielding to the prompting of the Holy Spirit from known sin varies with the individual. As a person grows older they are more tolerant of sin, and become less responsive to the Holy Spirit. Can one imagine, living nine hundred years, and how the mind would give way to perverted thoughts against the knowledge of God.

Today, life expectancy is approximately seventy years. Thus, the sooner one is exposed to the Gospel of Christ, the greater the probability of becoming Christian. Sunday school and seven day clubs are an absolute necessity for evangelism.

The events surrounding the separation of man from a Holy and Righteous God is attributed to original sin. The moment Adam and Eve ate the forbidden fruit they died spiritually, and being deceived into thinking they could be as little gods, their body began to die. A chemical, inherent in the forbidden fruit, triggered the process of death. The main weakness that is critical to longevity is the gene's inability to enable the body to process alcohol. (Beasley, 1987) Alcohol is oxidized from the body, never metabolized by the body. Oh, if we had known the consequence of sin.

Alcohol related events over history, demonstrate how the seed of Adam's loin contained a history altering state of the reproductive system. Adam passed along his likeness, and his image through the seed of his loin. (Genesis 5:3) God, not willing that man should perish, preserved the seed of the woman blameless to bring about the sinless Son of Man, a second Adam who knew no sin. (2 Corinthians 5:21) Since the resurrection of Christ a new generation of creatures is being generated and will soon populate the earth in co-habitation with God. (Genesis 3:15; Luke 1:26-35; Revelation 21:1-7)

There is a natural body and there is a spiritual body. The first Adam is a living soul, complete with progressive disintegration of the body. The second Adam is a quickening spirit, embodying the fullness of the Godhead, eternal in resurrection. The first Adam is of the earth and under judgment. The second Adam is the Lord Jesus Christ from heaven, even Jesus who is the Savior of humanity. (1 Corinthians 15:44b-50; Colossians 2:9)

The Fall of Man

The Genesis account describes the fall of man. It is important to note how sin, interacting in the natural body is prevented from interacting in the spirit. (1 Corinthians 2:14-16) Humans take pride in the flesh. They fashion a life style after the beautiful, and take pleasure in those who set the example for the world. (Romans 6:6; 1 John 5:18) The body and soul of the Christian is no different than the body and soul of a non-Christian. However, the spirit of the unbeliever is darkened before God; the spirit of the Christian is a new creature in Christ, and set before God.

The Christian spirit is not made righteous, but is a new creation. To make one righteous on earth is impossible. Adam's nature was proud. Some take pride in false humility; that is not humility. Jesus set Himself apart as Holy for the sake of the disciples, and for those who believe. (John 17:17-21) Righteousness is of the Lord.

Moses stood by Aaron as the Lord consumed Aaron's two sons by fire. Later, Moses explained to Aaron, "This is what the Lord has said, 'I will set myself in them that come near me, that I may be glorified before all the people." (Leviticus 10:1-3) Concerning sanctification, the Lord is concerned not only with His holiness, but the Christians as well. Christian holiness brings about sanctification, as set apart from the world, and set apart unto God. Through the indwelling Holy Spirit, the divine nature of Christ is imparted to the Christian. So, by nature, the Christian is sanctified as holy. (2 Cor. 5:21) A false sense of holiness can be experienced in the old nature, but it is a manifestation of the flesh. (Nee, 1972)

The desire for pleasure and the pride of life is cause to use alcohol and/or drugs. Drugs, even those prescribed by doctors, can give a sense of euphoria. When a pharmaceutical pain tablet is not available, the effect of whiskey is used to bring about pleasure, and help overcome bodily pain. It allows the natural body the ability to endure suffering by adjusting its tolerance and dependence levels. (Wadstein and Ohlin, n/d) The soul, when influenced by alcohol, enhances self-esteem.

The Alcohol Syndrome was the best-kept medical mystery of modern man. It was 1971 when medical scientists observed the abnormal growth of infants born to alcoholic mothers. In one survey, ninety seven percent of women used prescribed drugs. Many administered drugs to their bodies during pregnancy. (Fried, 1983) The unborn child absorbs these same drugs in adult strength. When the mother drinks, smokes, or take drugs, the baby drinks, smokes, and take drugs. The mystery behind the depravity of man is the extent to which biological damage comes upon the human fetus by alcohol.

In eighteenth century England, the British Parliament passed the famous "Gin Act" to curb the abuse of alcohol. The human toll alcohol took on Great Britain's new born children, was devastating. Medical records show seventy-five percent of Christened babies died before the age of five. These were babies born into normal families. Medical scientists concluded that it was a direct result of drinking too much whiskey and gin. (Fried, 1983) The "Gin Act" of Great Britain passed in 1738.

In a general population count taken from 1704 to the passing of the gin act, England's population decreased by 960,296 children. (Leeky, 1883) This number averages as seventy-seven (77) burials per day. Not counting those children older than the age of five.

History corroborates the cost of life and property as a direct result of drinking alcohol. Many, including Christians, disagree with its debilitating effects. Two out of three individuals, when asked about alcohol affecting the health of an individual said, "Most drinkers do not suffer health problems because of their drinking." At least half these people reason that moderate drinking is good for the health. (Eliany, 1989) Some medical doctors even suggest to their patients who drink in moderation, that alcohol may even improve their health. The mystery behind the secret of humanity's fall in the Garden of Eden is not so hard to understand. Anyone who would suggest before 1971, that drinking was harmful to health would be considered foolish.

The Deception

The best-kept secret behind the fall of man is, "The Alcohol Syndrome." However, many deny the significance it has upon the psyche of man. An examination for stress was conducted in Nova Scotia, Ca. Adolescents with drinking problems experienced greater stress. (Eliany, 1989) Within the makeup of the genetic code, stress shows more evidence of strain. Internal Medicine editorialize how, "the treatment of alcoholism has not improved in any important way in twenty five years." (Vaillant, 1983) Yet, medical doctors rationalize drinking in moderation in light of all this evidence.

The only way of helping those addicted to drugs and alcohol is to change their belief system. Otherwise, a lifetime of maintenance is required in support of their former belief system. (Vaillant, 1983) In a world where the pursuit of happiness is associated with the pride of life, and the desire for pleasure, it is difficult to find a substitute for alcoholism.

A belief system matures through the process of suffering. One can know, and one can identify with different belief systems. There is support; there is routine; there is enforcement; and there is hope. (Vaillant, 1983) For those who work with the addicted, many believe it necessary to deny access to the past, and so negate the recovery process. (Martin, 1987) Most Christians come from an addictive past: Many live within an addictive environment where rejection is an everyday experience. The rejection syndrome is a common characteristic in every sector of society.

The Suffering

Refusal of a foreign substance during the first trimester of pregnancy is most difficult. Morning sickness just won't go away. Though being aware and knowledgeable of birth defects, many will still take a drink, a drug, or smoke a cigarette through delivery. Until the kidneys are functional, and oxidize alcohol, the amniotic fluid enclosing the unborn child is for passing waste. The method is carried on for about six months. The fluid, while providing a safe environment for the child, inhibits the growth of bacteria guarding against harmful infection. Alcohol is oxidized from the unborn child in the same way it is in an adult, the liver. Until the liver is functional, and the kidneys are developed, the unborn child will suffer some degree of abnormality from the toxicity of alcohol.

During the first trimester an unborn child will also suffer effects from outside stress. Stress is caused by intense light, noise, or abnormal activity by the mother. Substance of a foreign nature will always cause physical suffering. The Fetal Alcohol Syndrome is the critical end of the spectrum for alcohol related sufferings. These signs are later identified as behavioral, learning, and delinquency. (Martin, 1987)

Scientists are looking for answers in the cellular structure of the brain. Recently, neurology professor Albert Galaburda of Harvard Medical School, and Dr. Thomas Kemper of the Boston City Hospital conducted landmark research on the brain of a dyslexic man who died in an accident. While the brain appeared perfectly normal to the naked eye, microscopic examination of thin slices of the brain revealed a general immaturity in the structure of the left side of the brain as well as the cells of its language centers. The doctors found gray matter cells in parts of the brain usually containing white mater, as well as a disordered arrangement of nerve cells in the cortex, or the brain covering. Because of such findings, Drs. Galaburda and Kemper, have concluded that profound differences may exist in the brains of dyslexics, which may be the result of some chemical abnormality during the early stage of fetal development. Such chemical aberrations, says Dr. Galaburda, may have a genetic history, which would explain why dyslexia often runs in families. (Ladies Home Journal, 1984)

Effects of dyslexia also cause symptoms of rejection. Dyslexia, as a genetic birth defect, affects the ability to read, write, spell, or memorize. Despite normal intelligence, intact sense organs, proper instruction, and normal motivation, many cannot cope. Dyslexia has many symptoms relating to language. The relationship between the central neuronal membranous pathway, and the function of hearing, create effectual noise to the listener. Thus, dyslexia causes degrees of poor communication that relates to social rejection. (Money, 1962)

Many social workers, pastors, and counselors, do not realize those clients, who suffer from communication problems, may be dyslexic. In a diagnostic of hearing and speech disorders, the range of disorders in communication come under four categories; a hearing impairment, speech articulation, voice problems, and language disorders. Infantile perseveration (cluttering) is where a six year old talks in patterns of a thirty-month old child. In its extreme form, marked omissions or substitution of sound and jargonic speech are factors relating dyslexia to cluttering. (Benton and Pearl, 1978)

Children who suffer from dyslexia experience an endless trail of rejection leading to alcoholism. To cope with rejection, the drinking usually begins about the twelfth year. Unless dealt with early in life, many could succumb to delinquency, and violent crime. In general, all who have poor communication skills, suffer extreme rejection. (Velton and Simpson, 1978)

Could it be that man forgot, or is ignorant of physical organic organization? Lodged in the shrine of their god-like nature, human beings think they can rid themselves of the shackles with which matter is invented. They scorn their physical being, and utterly ignore the reciprocal influences of their forbears in an urban interaction of mind and brain since the beginning of time. (Tuke, 1880) The Geneses account and the events that follow the fall of man attest to the statistical probability, that the fruit from the tree of the knowledge of good and evil, as in every other fruit, contained varying degrees in mg/kg amounts of alcohol.

The Genetics of the Fall

Dr. Henry Begleiter advanced the case for alcoholism, as a genetically transmitted disease. He focused his attention on young unborn children of alcoholics. He observed that thirty-five percent of alcoholic fathers produced alcoholic children. Most had mental and memory deficits, whereas less than one percent of a matched control group had the same pattern. (Emmett, 1978) Notice the focus is on the father, the one who fertilizes the egg, or seed of the woman. It is a fact that a significant sperm count is necessary to fertilize an egg. A woman, over her lifetime, will present an egg for fertilization approximately four hundred times. Strange as it may seem, but these four hundred eggs are already in the female child at birth.

Alcohol affects the central nervous system. Unfortunately, it does not always show for years. Many children perform consistently lower in academic achievement as in reading, writing, spelling, and arithmetic. (Fried, 1983) Dyslexia is a dysfunctional aspect of the brain and central nervous system, and is attributed to most learning and communication difficulties. (Brutten, et al, 1979) Both dyslexia and alcoholism are linked to feelings of stupidity, ugliness, and clumsiness, with feelings of inadequacy, insecurity, doubt, worry, and guilt that devastate the sufferer. As a result, many could be socially accepted individuals, withdraw from society, and the Church. Psychotherapy appears useless unless reinforced with frequent support meetings. (Levinson, 1994) Jesus said, "Take my yoke upon you, and learn of me; for I am meek and lowly in heart; and you shall find rest unto your souls, my yoke is easy, and my burden is light." (Matthew 11:28-30) Feelings, that are a direct result of rejection, contradict the Word of God.

Knowing what has transpired over millennia, the human mind has difficulty in knowing the will of God. Revival is not based on the ability or talents of man, but on the grace of God. He brings those He calls to a place of brokenness. The Cross is the answer to suffering and rejection. There is no better cure than the destruction of Adam's nature to sin. The old man is crucified with Christ, that the body of sin might be destroyed. (Romans 6:6) Surely, we must die to suffering!

The creationist account of the genesis of planets, and all things living, must be attributed to a loving God. It is impossible to uncover, or understand the nature and difficulties of a person's behavior other than illumination by the Holy Spirit. One must identify with "original" sin. Paul makes it clear in Romans Chapter Seven Verse Nine, "I was alive once without the law, but when the law came, sin revived and I died." Original sin separates from a loving God. Even though Paul believed he was in the will of God, original sin separated Paul from God while persecuting the early church. Jesus had to intervene on the Damascus road. (Acts 9:3-6)

How do we walk in the Spirit? Believe those things that bind us to the flesh are destroyed in Him who set us free in the Spirit. The Christian is not in bondage to the law of sin and death. The law of the Spirit of Life in Christ Jesus set us free. (Romans 8:1-4) God's judgment upon man is satisfied (propitiated) by the blood of Christ. His resurrection assures us that being justified by faith, we walk with peace in God through our Lord Jesus Christ. (Romans 4:25-5:1) To cover up the Genesis account is to deny the Word of God as factual, and preserved for generations.

Let us not think more highly of ourselves than we ought. Every Christian has been dealt the same measure of faith. As it was in Eden, so it is today, Satan has deceived many into thinking that God is to loving to condemn, and that He will never carry out His judgment. The Mystery of "Fallen Man" revealed in Genesis: The fact that substance abuse has attributed suffering to humanity; implies that ethanol was present in the forbidden fruit.

Those who suggest the battle for supremacy is between the old nature and the new nature are in error. The old nature is crucified with Christ. (Romans 6:6) The flesh and the Spirit are contrary one with the other so that we cannot always choose the things we should. To deny the Word of God is even scary. We have no peace, because we believe there is no peace. Believe not man, not woman, or any other word that denies the reality of God in creation, and the deity of Jesus Christ as being the only begotten of the Father.

Now you know how "sin" can be misunderstood among Christians. The chemicals found within our fruit and vegetables confirm the reality of ethanol. Could it be that countless thousands who are addicted to alcohol and drugs could be cured if only they knew of the source of "sin" in their members? Original "sin" is the substantiation of self in its desire to be like God. Christians, all too often search for peace and satisfaction through pills and drinking fruit from the vine. In the "Post-Reformation" period, we will find rest unto our soul, but don't count on it.

Chapter Six

Post Reformation

The last chapter showed how some would have us believe the Genesis account is not the cause for human suffering. Denial of the affects of the fall of man from a Sovereign God is the trappings of the Phenomenon of Deception. It is subtle and appealing; it plays with the mind, the emotions, and the will, together, they bring us into bondage. This requires a spiritual experience that restores the Church, and transforms the Christian belief system.

The Religious Experience

There is no instruction manual on how to be spiritual. There is no tool whereby one can be spiritually measured. Spirituality is a phenomenon that cannot be measured. The Protestant Reformation was a religious rebellion. It protested against the church for putting a price tag on sin. Evidence, of those who dared to measure God's Grace, brought forth tyranny in abstract concepts of religious experience, which became a wedge for indifference.

Reform has to do with concepts where reason doesn't quite cut it. Reason can never prove or disprove an absolute; rather it shows a range of probability of a concept being true or false, right or wrong, good or evil. Benjamin Disraeli once claimed there were three kinds of deception: lies, cursed lies, and statistics. Mark Twain suggested that after the facts are known, one should seek to distort them as much as possible. Stephen Leacock suggests that when gathering data, be prepared to fall back on the use of deceit. Create huge exaggerations, and fill the missing data with signs and wonders. Art emus Ward explained reason with the remark; "It ain't so much the things we don't know that gets us in trouble, but the things that we know that ain't so." (Class notes, Oxford Graduate School) Religious reform is difficult to prove as truth, and most humbling to admit to being wrong; it is a false and precarious concept.

The use of reform is used to redefine religious experience. Asking a person if they are saved is a foolish question if they do not know the meaning of the biblical term. It is a divisive question. Born again is a set of terms that show bias, and create division. Personal spiritual experience is difficult to express in words, to those who have not shared the same experience. Reform returns one to a form of reasoning that exaggerates the reality of personal religious experience.

Personal religious experience, explained with ecclesiastical terminology, is detrimental to the salvation experience. In most denominations, Christians learn to testify with words and expressions they hear from other Christians. It may be with words taken from the King James Bible as "thee" and "thou" and other such derivatives taken from old English. The Quakers and other Puritan movements were known to use these terms to appear more spiritual. These super Christians still gather in communities of believers to preserve their identity in religious experience.

Religion is a belief system with deep mystical experience. It must be explained in terms that are meaningful to those who do not share the experience. Revival is a spiritual manifestation. Most Christians never experience religion the same way. It threatens the loss of personal identity. It is easier to reform Church practice than to experience revival in its original format. Salvation through faith is a relationship between a loving God and repentant sinner. The effects of this relationship are transforming to the beholder.

The Protestant Reformers

Church reform began on October 31, 1517. A simple Monk by the name of Martin Luther protested certain practices of the Roman Catholic Church. He posted Ninety Five theses on the door of the All Saints Castle Church in Wittenberg, Germany. Luther's theses were a series of statements that attacked the sale of indulgences, a means of purchasing forgiveness of sin, practiced by the Roman Catholic Church. Luther was later excommunicated.

Indulgences were associated with the sacrament of penance. After one has confessed and repented of sin, they receive absolution by the priest. Provided, of course, they meet all the conditions. Sin is an act of disobedience before God. God forgives, and places the sin under the blood of Christ. This is the covering for sin, but the guilt of the offence must to be worked out in this life, or in an intermediate state of purgatory. Conditions to satisfy this guilt, is administered by priests, who act as mediators between the repentant sinner and God. They might lodge a pilgrimage to some shrine, or request a payment of money forwarded to the Church.

If the repentant sinner can pay, he receives a document that would free him from temporal penalty of guilt. It is believed by some that Christ, and the Apostles achieved merit points for their earthly ministry, and any excess of points is laid up in a heavenly treasury. These merit points could be withdrawn for the faithful. If necessary, a repentant sinner could even purchase a meritorious document on behalf of dead relatives. (Carins, 1996) The amount charged is determined by the repentant sinner's wealth and social position. Indulgences were free to the destitute, but a king or dignitary would pay heavily.

The reformation was both a pro-test for justification by faith and a protest against certain practices of the Roman Church. Primarily it was in opposition to the sale of indulgences. Many churches protested the practice all over Europe. The churches that protested did not all share the same theological stand. Many accepted the Bible as the final authority for practice and believed man did not need a priestly go-between to obtain salvation. (Carins, 1996) Within this protestant reform movement was a capitalistic middle class. They protested the drain of their wealth to the International Church under the Pope in Rome. They therefore, supported the movement, and helped in the establishment of the Protestant Church in Europe.

The Pattern of Reform

Meanwhile, on the other side of the Continent, Magellan's ship had already completed its maiden voyage around the world. The western hemisphere was open for settlement. The Protestant Church, from all theological persuasions, played a significant role in the work of discovering, settling, and actually exploiting the inhabitants of the New World under the banner of Christianity.

Church historians consider the Protestant Reformation a means by which the planting of Protestant Churches was patterned after the New Testament. Protestant reformers were anxious to develop a theology that was in complete accord with the authority of the Bible. Martin Luther was born of a peasant family, and studied philosophy and theology. His main emphasis was on the doctrine of Justification by Faith. The Protestant Church launched its mandate because this priest, Martin Luther, came to realize he was justified before God without the necessity of a human mediator.

The Anabaptist Church made the point of justification by adult baptism by immersion. Upon confession of Jesus Christ as Lord and Savior Christians, coming out of Roman Catholicism, were baptized again. Baptism as a child was annulled. Infant baptism does not allow for individual choice. Baptism by immersion is still practiced by most Evangelical Churches. This mode of baptism is believed to be similar to the Lord's baptism in the Jordan River. In some churches, baptism initiates the believer into Church membership.

Coming upon Jesus bodily in the form of a dove, the Holy Spirit confirmed Jesus' ministry, and God the Father spoke audibly from heaven declaring Jesus as His

Beloved Son. (Mark 1:9-11) Herein is evidence of the deity of Christ and the triunity, or three persons of the Godhead. Most Protestant Churches administer baptism in one mode or another as in sprinkling or dipping. Most evangelical churches have baptismal tanks. The more fundamental insist on a body of water such as a river or lake.

The Essentials

The Protestant Church is formed from three essentials. The first is to be a member of a universal worldwide institution. The second is that it be a worthy work. The third is competent leadership within the worldwide institution of Churches. The emerging protestant Church lost these essentials when they broke with the Roman Church. Establishing these essentials meant restructuring, or reformatting it's mandate as a church under God.

Ever since the Protestant Reformation, many have desired to establish unity within the Church on planet earth. A worldwide institution, organized between August 22 and September 4, 1948, initiated a new church age. The church could no longer claim Israel to be ancient history, nor substitute the church as the elect. Over 350 delegates, representing about 150 churches from 44 countries, met in Amsterdam and formed the World Wide Council of Churches. Two weeks earlier the American Council of Churches, and the National Association of Evangelicals organized the International Council of Christian Churches. Which of these institutions represent the Body of Christ? Protestants, Catholics, and Orthodox claim to be the Body of Christ. We, being many, are one body in Christ, and each a member of the other. (Romans 12:5)

The Head of the Church

One wonders what Christ had in mind when He mentions the unity of His Church. Did He have in mind a physical union, a spiritual union, or an invisible union wherein believers are placed in the body of Christ? Most organisms have a head. Christ is the head of His church. (Carins, 1996) A spiritual body is believed to be the most authentic. It is believed among some, that unless the Protestant Church returns to its former status under the Pope in Rome, it will not survive. Many believe that a revived Roman Church is on the horizon, and as such, a new order among many religions will form the new Church. It will emerge in cooperation with the new world order.

The Christian Church should not be seen as an institution. The Church is an organism consisting of components under the Headship of Jesus Christ. Revival, to live again, is the means by which believers, who make up the invisible Body of Christ, are united in His Death, Burial, and Resurrection. The Cross is the central vortex of this spiritual union.

The cross is a symbol of denying love of self. Jesus said, "If any man will come after me, let him deny self, by taking up his cross daily and following me. For by reason man will seek to save his life, and shall loss it; But should a man will (choose) to lose his life for my sake, the same shall save it." (Luke 9:23-24) Christians, preoccupied with sacraments, mixed with signs and wonders ordered by the institutionalized Church, will never experience true revival.

Many focus on Church sacraments and program venues for salvation. Resurrected life after death is not the norm for most Churches. Paul exclaims, “I am crucified with Christ; nevertheless I live; yet not I, but Christ lives in me: and the life which I now live in the flesh I live by the faith of the Son of God, who loved me, and gave Himself for me.” Again, “Are you so foolish; having begun in the Spirit, are you now made perfect by the flesh?” Who has betrayed you that you should not obey truth? Jesus Christ is clearly portrayed, and historically proven, as crucified. Think about it: Did you receive the Spirit by the works of the Law, or by the hearing of faith? Oh foolish Christian, what makes you think you can obtain perfection through works of the flesh? (Galatians 2:20; 3:1-3)

Jesus Christ does not change your life: He imparted a new Life. The new Life in the believer does not belong to the recipient; it is eternal Life in Christ. The believer never receives a gift of spiritual life that is his possession to manipulate. God the Holy Spirit is an entity who indwells our spirit. (McConkey, 1997) God the Father, God the Son, and God the Holy Spirit are One. (1 John 5:7-8) It is not just an imparting, it is not just an imputing, but it is the bringing about of a Life that quickens (administers) the body of the believer. (Romans 8:11) The Spirit of Christ, given of the Father, is that Holy Spirit who indwells the Christian by Faith. The new creature (new “me”) dwells in Christ, in heaven, waiting on the earnest (purpose) of our final inheritance, the redemption of the purchased possession (body) unto the praise of His Glory. (Ephesians 1:13-14) This is the whole, and must be taken factually.

.

The Rebellion

Rebellion is a sin against God's authority. Obedience is not so hard to learn. It is an act of God. The act upon which God showed His power was in raising Jesus from the dead. God raised Jesus from the dead, because the task of redemption was complete. Jesus said, "It is finished." God raised Jesus from the dead because the Christian is delivered from sin. So, just as God raised Jesus from the dead, He raises the Christian unto resurrected life after death in Christ. (Romans 4:22-5:1; 2 Corinthians 5:21; Ephesians 1:8-9) This is justification by faith in obedience, and establishes the promises revealed in resurrection.

If a Christian agrees to repent they have peace with God. The Christian is forgiven of sins past, sins present, and sins future. God is willing to release His Spirit of faith to whosoever wills to believe. (Colossians 2:13-14) The individual, being dead in sin, is revived as a new creature without sin in Christ. Forgiven of all unrighteousness, he is declared without sin in Christ. (John 7:16-18; Hebrews 8:12; 1 John 1:9) Further confession is unnecessary.

Peace is perfected in Christ. The Christian walks in the Spirit. Resurrection is confirmation of God's satisfaction. Christ's redemptive work is complete; it is finished. (Hebrews 4:1-12) God justifies the believer on the reality of resurrection. The Christian's life is hid with Christ, in

God, and sealed, by promise, until Christ, who is our Life, appears in Glory. (Ephesians 1:4-14; Colossians 3:1-4) Bodily redemption takes place when Christ returns in clouds of the air, and receives His Bride in the air. (1 Thessalonians 4:13-18) This is His final hour.

The Fruits of Rebellion

Martin Luther, while planting the Protestant Church in Europe, two notable men took a rebellious stand. In Wittenberg, Germany, Nicholas Storch and Mark Stubner claimed to have received an extra measure of God's grace, an extra measure of the Holy Spirit, and took extra matters into their hands. They believed they were called to bring about an immediate return of Christ, to abort the rapture, and to set up His physical Kingdom on planet earth.

These men were prophets or apostles of Zwickau. They taught concepts similar to the Anabaptists, but with extreme overtones. The Kingdom of God would appear on earth physically in their generation and that followers of the movement would have special revelations. However, at the risk of his life, Martin Luther returned to Wittenberg and overthrew the prophets and their radical teachings. (Carins, 1996)

Unfortunately today, there is no Martin Luther to lead the Church back to the reality that the just shall live by faith, and not by works of the flesh. So, what causes a leader to seek apostleship? It must be some spiritual interface that requires no accountability. One, when they begin to reason apart from the Word of God, can fall under a rebellious spirit, and produce fruits of unrighteousness.

These Zwickau prophets claim to have extra biblical revelation. Together they reasoned there was more to the reformation than Church planting and salvation by faith. They not only rebelled against the delegated authority of the Church, they rebelled against the authority of God. (Galatians 5:17)

Like the above, there have always been extremists. Not all Churches can be accused in whole or in part, as belonging to any extremist group. Paul evoked from Timothy, to lay hold of the gift. This gift of faith is for the believer. It is necessary for salvation, and to believe the Word of God. Christians, while prisoners of the Lord, share sufferings, and glory in resurrection. (1Tim. 4:14-15; 2 Timothy1:6-9) Christians identify with one another in co-crucifixion, co-burial, and co-resurrection in Christ. (Romans 6: 3-6)

The traditional Church fathers brought a theology of reform not transform. Passed down from generation to generation reform adds to, takes away from, and fits the Word in defense of some theological persuasion. This always leads to segregation. The Christian, to cast down imaginations and every high thing that exalts itself against the knowledge of God, must bring forth into captivity every thought to the obedience of Christ. This is the norm for the mature Christian. (2 Corinthians 10:5) It is clear from this passage that reason is in opposition to the knowledge of God. Reason seeks to justify a theological concept even when inconsistent with the Word of God.

The Results of Revival

Revival is to live again in resurrected life after death. It is a new structure built from new material. Matthew, Mark, and Luke, all record what Jesus said about redressing the old to have it look like something new. Jesus said, “No man puts a piece of new cloth unto an old garment for it makes the tear worse than before, nor do men put new wine into old bottles for the bottles will break, but they put new wine into new bottles that both the wine and the bottles are preserved.” (Matthew 9:16-17; Mark 2:21; Luke 5:36-38) We are new creatures, created in Christ.

Religious experience and church reform is an attempt to practice revival. Spiritual rebellion within the organized church will never bring a world awakening. It is not the intent to suggest that all churches are rebellious, and endorse strange phenomenon, but to practice revival is not the same as being revived. Some church leaders are filled with covetousness, and lead their followers to interpret revival as being some sort of hyper-religious experience. To what degree has the Church conformed to religiosity?

Post reformation spoke of reform, change for the better, do not indulge in sin, but rather dispute it. How the protestant reformation became established was not so much an act of faith, but an act of charity by those who were tired of giving their tithe to the Roman Church. It was an action of works rather than faith. Even though Martin Luther saw that justification by faith denied the need for a human mediator, it soon became the norm to come under a church composed of some community ethic and good works. Now, when it comes to transformation, faith becomes the mode for living. As you will see in the next chapter, the “Power of Transformation” faith and works become integrated in a community of grace.

CHAPTER SEVEN

POWER IN TRANSFORMATION

The Orthodoxy

Theology has destroyed all hope for church restoration. "Of all the reasons why unity has never characterized Christianity as a religious group is their inability to agree on what it means to be Christian." (Lazenby, Classnotes) The right to disagree is nurtured using a concept of orthodoxy. To be politically correct, one must conform to the beliefs, attitudes, and modes of conduct of some acceptable denominational theology.

Practical orthodoxy is brought about to explain Christian theology. Christians must consent to a common system of belief. It is suggested that if all Christians held the same view toward doctrines, Christian unity would become the norm. However, the church has yet to be restored.

Historical events have added insult to injury. The church is in defeat. It has failed in its mandate to teach what Jesus taught, and to baptize in the name of the Father, and the Son, and of the Holy Ghost. Rather it has chosen its own path, even to baptize in the name of Jesus only. It opened the way of eternal life to all religions, and forgotten that Jesus is the Way, the Truth, and the Life. No one comes to the Father, but by Him. He came to seek, to save, and to present the Christian as heirs of God, and joint-heirs with the risen Christ. (Romans 8:17)

Now, after more than two thousand years of debate, the inherent problem of correctness is obvious. Instead of a foundation to identify the inherent hope of Christianity in resurrection, the degree of correctness tends to encourage further division among the Christian Community. Each Christian should determine the correctness of a doctrine. Unfortunately, individuals approach doctrinal issues from a variety of cultural orientations. Full agreement on what doctrines, and what practices are correct, is impossible.

One Lord, one faith, one baptism is now more of a cliché than affirmation of faith and solidarity. Any correctness available to Christians today is lost in rhetoric. Doctrinal practice alone cannot identify a true Christian. If only, there were even one identity common to some, then the Christian Community may find agreement. (Lazenby Class notes)

The disciples of Jesus held many things common. They believed Jesus really was the Christ. They sold their possessions and goods, they distributed as every person had need, and they sought to preach the gospel. This practice was expected. To do otherwise was rebellion against the authority of God.

There was however, one instance of rebellion mentioned. A man and his wife were stricken to die, because they held back a portion of goods for themselves. (Acts 2:45; 5:1-10) The correctness of identifying all things common was carefully administered among the early Christians.

The Identification

Identification is important for theological correctness. The early Church stood firm when it came to being in Christ. The symbolism attributed to the crucifix displayed within the Catholic Church and in many Catholic homes show Jesus on the cross. The body and blood of Jesus is the foundation of Roman Catholic Theology. The Eucharist is the chosen pattern showing the body and blood of Christ. Jesus Christ is not identified before God for His physical appearance or His shed blood, but in His resurrection.

There are a number of historical writers who mention Jesus of Nazareth as a historical person. Tacitus, the Dean of the Roman historians, links the name and origin of Christians with Christus, who in the reign of Tiberius suffered death by the sentence of Pontius Pilate. Pliny, who was proprietor of Bithynia and Pontus in Asia Minor, wrote to the Emperor Trajan about 112 AD for advice as to how he should deal with Christians, who sing a song to Jesus as if to a God. Lucian wrote a satire on Christians and their faith about 170 AD. He described Jesus as one crucified in Palestine because he began a new cult. Lucian ridiculed the Christian for worshipping a crucified sophist or teacher of a cult.

The most notable of Jewish historians was Josephus. He was a wealthy Jew who sought to justify Judaism to the cultured Romans. He mentions James in his writings as a brother of Jesus, the so-called Christ. Josephus wrote of Jesus as a wise man condemned to death on the Cross by Pilate. (Carins, 1996) There is no question concerning the evidence of a historical Jesus of Nazareth. Jesus the

Christ was raised from the dead after three days. The theology of Jesus Christ would be taken to be the sign of Jonah, His resurrection from the dead. (Matthew 12:39; 27:63; Luke 11:30; Mark 8:31) How then, or of what symbol can best identify His resurrection?

Consider again for a moment, the account given in Scripture concerning the tree of the knowledge of good and evil. Prior to Adam and Eve eating its fruit, it was uniquely identified as the tree adjacent to the tree of life in the middle of the garden. It stood out because of its place in the middle of the garden.

Upon eating of its fruit, their eyes of reason were opened, and understanding their nakedness, sewed fig leaves for a covering, and hid among the other trees throughout the garden. (Genesis 3:8) Picture a naked man and a woman, dashing back and forth among the trees in a garden. God called to them from within the garden. They came with leaves strapped across their thighs. They could no longer be identified by their nakedness, but by their disobedience before a disappointed God.

The Christian is clothed in the resurrected Christ. The Lord looks upon them as being at rest; even as a loving parent would look upon a sleeping child. Must we appear before the Judgment Seat of Christ, and give account to the things done in the body? There is a contrasting "but" that shows we are made manifest (naked) before God, and also in the consciousness of our peers. (2 Corinthians 5:10-11) As Christian, there is no fear in judgment. We are called to stand (naked) in Christ, and give testimony unto the world clean from a consciousness of shame.

According to the Genesis account, after Adam and Eve ate of the fruit of the tree of knowledge of good and evil, God executed His judgment upon Adam and Eve. They lost their spiritual identity. They could no longer stand in the midst of the garden without shame. They took upon themselves the identity of an earthen vessel. Disobedient before God, the serpent had tricked them, and the inequity of sin became symbiotic with their nature. Yes, a parasite to feed upon their mind, body and the emotions. (Galatians 5:17) The natural man cannot experience things of the Spirit of God. Salvation is a foolish concept. Paul, in his natural state, persecuted the Christian. That is, until his body was struck blind. Then, having lost his ability to see, he was identified and led as a child. After his eyes were opened, he preached Christ Risen from the dead. Paul then identified with the resurrected Christ. (Acts 9:1-20)

The Mind of Christ

The Scriptures teach the Christian has the Mind of Christ. Adam lost his identification when he disobeyed God. Being born again simply means to pass from death unto life. When the spirit of man identifies with the Holy Spirit of God in resurrection, he is no longer a sinner. The judgment on sin is complete. (Romans 8:1, 33-34) The natural mind dare not question the testimony of a Christian. If they did, it would be a mockery of God's grace. The most a Christian could say in defense is, the Lord rebuke you. (Jude 1:8-9) There is no judgment coming upon the Child of God.

The Christian need never to fear the wrath of God. The

Christian, accessing the Mind of Christ in resurrection, is their identification of a Christian's place under the control, and authority of Father God. (Genesis 5:3; Romans 8:1-2; 1 Corinthians 2:14-16; Colossians 3:1-17) The Mind of Christ identifies the hope of a Christian as, "Christ in you, the hope of glory." (Colossians 1:27)

The Authority

God must honor His Word. He executed judgment upon Adam, Eve, the environment, earth, and all creatures, especially the serpent. Under the influence of Satan, the serpent caused Eve to question her knowledge of God. God placed Eve under the authority of her husband, but she did not make enquiry. The fact that a woman is responsible in bearing the seed of a man implies man's authority over the woman. The ground is cursed to bring forth fruit from labor which mankind must work by the sweat of his brow. (Genesis 3:1-19) Satan was created as an anointed Cherub. (Ezekiel 28:1-19) This creature was beautiful, perfect in all his ways, and served the living God until the sin of iniquity entered his heart.

As an anointed Cherub, Satan rebelled against the authority of God, and lost his identity. God executed judgment upon Satan, the prince of this world referred to as the devil. (John 16:10) He is identified as the commander and chief over the seed of Adam. Jesus referred to the father of the Jews as being of the devil. (John 8:31-47) It is clear that God did not negate His judgment upon fallen angels, but what of the human race? Check out the graveyard to see the effects of God's judgment. Unless there be a way to pass from death unto life, all shall perish. Yet, it is not God's will that any person perish. He provided a way of escape. He caused His only begotten Son Jesus to be the Way, the Truth and the Life. He subjects all persons unto eternal damnation, except those in Christ. (John 3:16-18)

The Preserved Seed

The word "seed" is emphasized in the creation account because it is the "seed" of the woman, not the "sperm" of man that accounts for the birth of Christ. A young virgin girl, betrothed to marry a man whose name was Joseph. Her name was Mary. The angel Gabriel was sent to inform her that she would conceive in her womb a Son, and shall call His name Jesus. He continued to say, "The Holy Spirit will come upon you, and the power of the Highest will overshadow you; therefore, also, that Holy One who is to be born will be called the Son of God." (Luke 1:26-37) The seed of the woman is preserved unto salvation, while the sperm of the man is the progeny of sin.

Conceived of the Holy Spirit, Jesus of Nazareth was without sin. God came into the world at the conception of Jesus. Who can dispute the beginning of life for the human child? Jesus said: "Sacrifice and offering you did not desire, but a Body have you prepared for Me. In burnt offerings and sacrifices for sin, You had no pleasure." Then He said, "Behold I have come - In the volume of the book it is written of me - To do your will, O God." Jesus became the perfect "sin sacrifice" in judgment of Adam's transgression to make a new generation wherein dwells the "righteousness" of God in Christ. This is the Christian.

It is because of the Second Advent, the seed, preserved in the woman that Mary conceived the Son of God, the Man Christ Jesus, our Savior and Lord. In Christ Jesus, the Christian becomes the new chosen generation, a royal priesthood, a holy nation, a peculiar people, those called out of darkness into His marvelous light; the people of God. (1 Peter 2:9-10) It is through Jesus' birth, death, burial, and resurrection that we are passed from death unto life. (Hebrews 10:5-10; 1 John 3:14) Jesus Christ, as being the firstborn among the dead, and we being raised to new life, are brethren after the order of Melchizedec. (Romans 8:29; Genesis 14:18; Psalm 110:4)

Two people dwell on planet earth. A generation of Adam who dwell in bondage to sin whose soul and spirit are separated from God, and a Christian generation who are empowered by the Holy Spirit in victory over sin, whose spirit and life are integrated in Christ. These generations of two peoples dwell together on planet earth.

In Christ, Christian brethren all dwell in unity of the Spirit. As clear as this may be, resentment amidst Christians on earth, grow stronger by the moment. The world watches as we tear each other apart. (1 Corinthians 6:5-8) Though no longer thrown to the lions, but because we fail to identify with the resurrected Christ in a bond of peace, and being clothed in earthen vessels, we make war on one another. With no cost to the world, we become as fools.

Jesus Christ, having abolished in His flesh the enmity of sin and the law through obedience, He made of Himself a new generation of man, so making peace. (Romans 5:17-

19) He reconciled unto God one body by the Cross, having slain the enmity between Jew and Gentile, He speaks to those both near and far, yet peace is not evident among the brethren. (Ephesians 2:14-22) The Christian Church cannot fulfill its mandate, until Christians identify with Jesus in His death, burial, and resurrection. Christian, we are brethren, the very seed of Christ, who is the seed of Abraham, who is the seed of God. (Acts 13:23; Romans 9:5-14; Galatians 3:19-22; Hebrews 2:16-18, 29)

The Church Divided

Many Christians hold to the Reformed Protestant faith of John Calvin (1509-1564). Other Christians hold to a Reformed Protestant faith of James Arminius (1560-1609). Calvin funded his training from within a professional legal class. The education of Arminius, funding came through friends, and later by civic authorities of Amsterdam. (Carins, 1996) These men, elevated to ecclesiastical fame for their theology, were from two levels of society. The rich and poor, the educated and the learned, are both brethren in the Lord.

One was raised and educated within a wealthy upper middle class, and the other raised and educated in a lower middle class. James Arminius came on the scene sixty years after the theology of John Calvin was established in the Church. Arminius disagreed with some of Calvin's opinions on election, and so determined to modify Calvin's system of beliefs to fit a less orthodox form of theology. It is unfortunate that Calvin did not have opportunity to debate. He died when Arminius was only four years old.

However, over the past five hundred years, these two belief systems have been debated with such intensity, they divide the Christian Church. The social class, of these two giants of the faith, is not the issue. It is in not knowing, and in not being sure on whose authority the Christian is called. Is it a judicial position of a Church, or the authority of a loving God? Can one be called faithful outside the church, or must all enter into the covenant of the church?

In brief, both men taught that mankind inherited Adam's sin, and are subject to the wrath of God. However, these are thoughts that came from men who pay homage to reason. In other words, if everybody has an opinion, where then comes the authority of God? Since John Calvin died in 1564 and James Arminius in 1609, the King James Bible (printed in 1611) could not be blamed for the controversy they brought to Christianity.

Calvin thought, being inherently evil, mankind was unable to initiate salvation. No man seeks after God. (Romans 3:11) After God grants grace, man wills to cooperate with the Holy Spirit. Arminius, on the other hand thought, being inherently good man is enabled for salvation. After God grants grace, man then wills to cooperate.

Calvin thought, some were chosen to salvation, while others were left to perish. This was conditional on God knowing beforehand who would accept Grace and be saved, and who would refuse Grace and be condemned. Arminius also thought, some were chosen to salvation, with others left to perish. This was unconditional of God knowing who would accept Grace and be saved, and who would refuse His Grace and be condemned.

Calvin thought God gave Saints grace not to fall back under the judgment of original sin. The carnal man is given over to Satan, but not to damnation. (1 Corinthians 5:5) Calvinists teach it is impossible for Christians to lose their salvation. Arminius thought, if God gave Saints grace not to fall back under the judgment of original sin, it would imply that man is without choice. This would show God as the author of sin. Armenians teach, if a Christian would deny the moving of the Holy Spirit, and be disobedient to their calling, they could lose their salvation, and be in danger of eternal damnation. (Mark 3:30)

Theology is an outward expression of an inward thought based on the knowledge of God. These are concepts on which God distributes His Divine Grace. If rationale has its way, thoughts, when in opposition to the knowledge of God, are most difficult to submit to the obedience of Christ. (2 Corinthians 10:5) Let no one think they deserve anything from the Lord, for that one would be unstable. (James 1:7-8) Theology is the study of God's Word. For those who believe the Bible contains error, it is dangerous to contend outside the revealed Word of God. (Matthew 21:23-27; Mark 11:28-33; Luke 20:1-8)

James and John, the sons of Zebedee, came unto Jesus contending they should sit one on the left hand and one on the right hand of Jesus in His Glory. Jesus replied, "You know not what you ask of me. Are you able to drink the same cup I drink, and are you able to survive the same baptism I must undergo, perhaps you shall; But to sit on my right hand or my left hand is not mine to give, but it is for them for whom it is prepared." (Mark 10:35-45) Now, when the other ten disciples heard, they were filled with indignation and resented James and John for thinking they were more favored than the rest. Could John Calvin or James Arminius have ever imagined how their contention affected the Christian Church? We are divided, we are filled with indignation and resentment, and we are driven to question the authority of God's Word.

The Cup and Baptism

How serious will be the judgment upon those who grapple over God's Word with hands of clay? We fear God only as we fear the fire of hell, and that is also in question. To represent God is not an easy thing; it is too great and too marvelous for one to touch. One needs to walk strictly in the way of obedience. The path for all Christians is obedience, not to question the Living Word; Christians are servants not leaders; we are slaves not rulers. (Nee, 1972)

Apostles, James and John were sons of Zebedee, both unsure of their position. Theologians, James and John were founders of Arminianism and Calvinism, both unsure of their position. Neither knew the significance of the cup that Jesus drank, nor could they imagine the effects of the baptism that Jesus underwent. Must we drink of the cup and undergo the baptism? Indeed, we are crucified with Christ, but must we suffer the wrath of God? We were baptized (placed) into His death on the cross. We were buried in Christ, and raised to new life.

Come with me to the Garden of Gethsemane and listen as the Lord prayed over the options laid before Him:

"My Father, if it be possible, let this cup pass from me: nevertheless, not as I will, but as you will." Notice the cup would not be removed, and would not be altered. It was fixed. After three supplications, Jesus proclaimed, "The cup which the Father has given me to drink, I must drink." This sacrificial cup was poured out upon Jesus. Please, the Word of God demands obedience. God's will is more important than circumstance. Taking the cup to drink meant Jesus' submission to the judgment of God in obedience. Sin must be put away once and for all. The Father looked away as His only begotten Son Jesus was sacrificed on the cross. Those who are obedient to God must comply with His will, and take up their cross and follow Jesus. (Luke 9:23) The old man is crucified with Christ. (Galatians 2:20) The Christian must not disobey the Word of God. There are no other options whereby we can be saved from the wrath of God that comes upon the children of disobedience. (Ephesians 5:6) (Nee, 1972)

In evidence of obedience, and the need for sacrifice, God tested Abraham. God asked him to take his son Isaac and offer him for a burnt offering. The next day Abraham arose in obedience, took some wood, a couple of men, and his son. He took the wood and placed it upon his son. Now, Isaac was concerned. He saw the wood, he saw the fire, and he saw the knife, then he made the enquiry, "Father, where is the lamb?"

Abraham assured him that God would provide. Three days later Isaac, yet being obedient to his father, was bound and laid upon the wood on a stone alter. Then, taking the knife, Abraham raised it over the lad in preparation to kill, but at that moment, the Angel of the Lord called unto him out of heaven and said, “Abraham, Abraham:” and he answered, “Here I am.”

The Angel of the Lord said, “Lay not your hand upon the lad, neither do anything unto him: For now I know that you fear God, seeing you have not withheld your son, your only son from me.” Abraham released Isaac, looked up toward a thicket where a ram was entangled by its horns in the branches. Abraham took the ram, killed it, and gave it in sacrifice. Isaac, his only son, was spared.

As a result of Abraham’s obedience, God promised that He would multiply his seed as the stars of heaven and as the sand of the sea. The same covenant was renewed with Isaac’s son Jacob. Jacob’s name was changed to Israel. It is in this name, that the nations of the earth are blessed. (Genesis 22:1-18)

The Angel of the Lord is a Christophany, an appearance of Jesus before He came in the flesh as the Christ Child. This shows the Deity of Christ. It was the will of Father God, that Jesus, His only begotten Son, would be the Lamb of sacrifice. There was no other that could redeem mankind from the wrath of God. The baptism Jesus endured on the cross was this sacrificial death. Howbeit then, that being placed into His death, mankind can appropriately take up the cross and identify with Jesus in His death, burial, and resurrection. His death as the sacrificial Lamb of God is well documented throughout the entire Holy Bible. (John 1:29, 35; Revelation 21:27)

Jesus anticipated life after death. The blessing of God in Christ was held back until death was accomplished.

This means, life after death is in anticipation of the atonement for sin. Life and atonement for sin became one in Christ. Jesus, in all His fullness, released Life unto death through the cross, and took it up again in resurrection. Kindled as a fire cast upon the earth, God's eternal Life, Christ's life, burns through the embers to whosoever will, in obedience to the Word of God, and act in accordance to His Will.

We are crucified with Christ. As a kernel of grain must die before its life can emerge, so too, the Christian must take their place together with Christ on the Cross. No one can atone for one's own sin. The blood of Jesus is the only atonement for sin. The imparting of eternal Life in resurrection is the effect of atonement. Jesus' sacrifice, as the Lamb of God, satisfied God's judgment for sin. The Christian reckons their old life in Adam as crucified. The life we live on earth is by the faith of Jesus, and carried out in the power of the Holy Spirit. This is our victory.

The Gift of Faith

Spiritual life is based on that measure of faith. It restores the Christian soul via the Spirit. Grace is the unmerited favor of God measured in proportion to obedience in the will of God. To live in resurrected life after death, one must know Jesus as Lord, and to experience His power through obedience in the Holy Spirit. The gift of grace through faith never binds, but releases one unto victory.

Whether or not one can lose their salvation will never be known. In all certainty, it is not for mortals to decide. Reason, on the basis of speculation, is rebellion against the Word of God. Jesus made it clear to John and James, the sons of Zebedee, that He did not have the authority to assign those who sit on His right hand or on His left. Obedience through faith is the essence of God's authority.

The Christian lives through faith and hope, but it is love that constrains them to be Christ-like. Until one knows authority, love is impossible. Agreement on doctrines and practices are beyond reason. One Lord, one Faith, one Baptism, can only attest to solidarity in Christ. There is no traditional concept of correctness available that Christians can affirm true orthodoxy. Doctrinal considerations alone but identify a belief system. Only, when one attests to life after death, can the assurance of unity be realized.

Those who look to Jesus for eternal life will not lack the blessing of Abraham. However, those who look for blessings, baptisms, signs, and wonders are in danger of keeping their life, but to lose it for the sake of Christ is to be at peace. To suffer, spend, and to be spent for Christ, is a reversal of the deep-rooted, controlling principle of the carnal human heart. The principle of self-love can only be experienced in resurrected life. (McConkey, 2005)

A community of grace is common to all Christians who confess Jesus Christ as Savior and Lord. It is true that many are conformist, and believe in an orthodox church, but to others it may not be an acceptable community. This chapter established the basis and power of transformation to all who believe. The scriptures tell us not to be conformed, but to be transformed by the renewing (restructuring) of the mind. (Romans 12:2) Even so, you will find in the next chapter, "Anarchy within the Body" seems to prevail.

Chapter Eight

Anarchy Within the Body

Tolerance: A Compromising Wedge of Indifference.

Christians, in their obsession with works in serving the Lord, take on too much responsibility. They take on the responsibility of a society without regulation. This is anarchy. Living in a state of forgotten promises, the Church stands against the authority of God. Commitment is weakened by tolerance. Agreement on doctrine and practice is necessary for service. One Lord, one Faith, and one Baptism could provide solidarity, wherein church revival may be forthcoming. The theology of Calvin and Arminius hold strong influence in today's social gospel. Though debated with intensity, there is mere tolerance. There is no agreement between church denominations.

Tolerance, without debate, can bring revival. It brought together Charles Finney, Peter Cartwright, Theodore Frelinghuysen, Jonathan Edwards, Samuel Davis, George Whitefield, and a host of others as leaders in revival. These personalities emerged from both camps and seemed tolerant of their theological differences. One family, John Wesley and his brother Charles were leaders of a Holy Club. Through methodical Bible study, prayer habits, and attempts to provide social service in jails, and in homes of the poor, they became known as the Methodists. (Carins, 1996) Methodists are known for being zealous of works.

William Booth (1829-1912) was a Methodist preacher. His zeal for the lost among the slums of East End London grew into a work known today as The Salvation Army. The Salvation Army is a church organization. It began as a Christian Mission without the inclusion of the sacraments of baptism or the Lord's Supper. Today, many Corps officers seek identification through Church association. Ironically, the Salvation Army is not a denomination.

Denominations are tolerant of sacraments. The Salvation Army is Methodist with Arminian theology. Officers warn membership that if they want to remain in the church, they must abstain from gambling, alcohol, and drugs. They insist on each signing a petition, and if one falls back into sin they are forbidden to wear the uniform, or lead in Corps Council. If recovering from drugs or alcohol, the fear of losing their salvation keeps them sober.

Similar Para-Church organizations have formed over the years. They seek to remain non-denominational to fit with those who are geared to theological persuasions. Most Para-Church groups like Youth for Christ, Intervarsity Christian Fellowship, and Youth with a Mission, involve church evangelism. The Canadian Revival Fellowship, Dynamic Churches International, Freedom in Christ, and Grace Fellowship International, are organizations involved in church discipleship. All service the need of the Church in revival, but compromise their witness in theology.

Organizations involved in evangelism and discipleship exist for those Churches interested in bringing converts into membership. Organizations involved in revival exist for Churches interested in delivering Christians from bondage. Both are wake up calls for the Christian Church. These ministries are inter-denominational or non-denominational in scope, and cannot be identified by orthodox theology.

Revival ministries stand clear from issues of theology and are trans denominational. Some who come forward in a Protestant evangelistic campaign may be referred to the Roman Catholic Priest for counsel and discipleship. Para-church organizations are the result of tolerance between the Christian faith, and other sects of Christianity, but not true to any form of orthodoxy. Most work under the banner of non-denominational faith missions.

The Fallacy of Works

James, the brother of Jesus, wrote to the twelve tribes of Israel, saying, "Can any one say of another, you have faith, and I have works: show me your faith without your works, and I will show you my faith by my works." (James 2:14-20) Is this much the same issue that plagues Arminian and Calvinistic theology? Is it a work of Grace, or is it a work of faith? The controversy is between faith and works. It is of faith when the Christian trusts in God. Is it of works, when men and women masquerade as ministers of good? The latter tremble because they are judged by their works. It is meaningless rhetoric, to think that one would argue that faith without works is dead. It is by grace we are saved through faith. We are justified by faith, not by works. (Matthew 8:28-32; Mark 5:1-13; Luke 8:26-33)

Many Churches are serious under their mandate for social service. Faith movements are effects of religious/political zeal. This appears to be the order of good works. Their mandate is based on the belief that faith without works is dead. Therefore, Arminians have a condition for works. Recall, James Arminian was born into a family of a deprived social class, whereas John Calviin was born into a family of wealthy professionals. James was a peasant and John was a lawyer. Is the real issue before us a matter of faith and works, or the poor and the wealthy? There are few Christian service organizations that do not have their hands out to the government for money. Is this faith that works? Most Christian groups are of works, and tolerant of each other in their mandate in serving the Lord.

Once in a small village, a woman named Martha asked Jesus to stop by for a time of fellowship. Martha had a sister Mary who rested at Jesus' feet listening as He spoke the Word of God. Martha, overly preoccupied in serving the evening meal, became annoyed. After a time, she came to Jesus and asked adamantly, if He did not care that her sister had left her to serve all alone. Tell her Lord, she pleaded, to come and help me serve. Jesus answered her by telling how she was overly concerned with serving, when only one thing was necessary. That was to listen to the Word. Her sister Mary had chosen the latter. (Luke 10:38-42) Jesus was tolerant of Martha's request. Mary could share the burden of serving, but she was receiving the Word of the Lord whereas Martha lost out on learning of Him who loved her. (Matthew 11: 28-30)

So many workers do share the same reward. Why work hard, if the reward is not forthcoming? Those involved in social ministry want praise of men. When praise is not forthcoming, they take on more programs. The reward is taken for granted by those who do not get involved. Most social services, are over flowing with work, and keep asking for more workers and volunteers. What is the focus in the story of Mary and Martha? Jesus was focused on faith, not on works. Jesus has no tolerance for works when it comes to faith; He chose Mary for her faith.

The Breakdown

When a theology of works fails to bring change, the tactic is to regroup. During the stage of regrouping, enterprising young zealots will often pick up on the failed cause, particularly when it is about social change. On the 15th of May, 1876, a young man of twenty-five chaired the first meeting of an Ethical Cultural Movement. Felix Adler, a young Jew, set out to form the first religious society based on the supreme worth of the individual. He avoided all formal creeds, sacraments, and theology that would identify the movement with the Church. He put forth a focus on a work of ethics. (Ericson, 1988)

Putting the focus on ethics, workers are responsible to develop a personal position of human faith. Ethical movements emphasize the importance of spiritual values, moral creativity, ethical democracy, and social consciousness for life. Ethical movements come forward because traditional forms of religion fail in meeting the needs of individuals and society. Ethical religion, humanistic in focus, is vogue in today's society. The cliché "I am only human" identifies an ethical humanistic belief system in many contemporary Church Movements.

Rick Warren leads a movement of ethics to bring about world peace. To accommodate working with people of all faiths, Warren has posited an acronym for peace. P is for (P)romoting reconciliation, E is for (E)quipping ethical leaders, A is for (A)ssisting the poor, C is for (C)aring for the sick, and E is for (E)ducating the next generation. Rick Warren switched from a religious focus to a political focus. He originally had the acronym for P and E as (P)lanting churches, and (E)quipping leaders. Faith failed to meet his mandate for society, and switched to works.

Sigmund Freud had profound influence on developing a pattern for twentieth-century Church Movements. An individual's self-esteem demanded dignity, equality, recognition of goals, and expectation of reward. Freud was convinced that people created a god in the image of their father. God was no more, or no less than an exalted father in the mind of most including the Christian. Christian psychology, filled with nuances that build upon low self-esteem, is the basis for self-help literature. Somewhere in the past, parental love was absent and experienced rejection. Self-esteem became their focus in life. (Justice, 1984)

Those who are influenced by the Freudian view of life believe that by the age of eight a child forms an image of the personality of the father. The serving medium adds servings of inherited images, mysteriously passed from generation to generation, topped off with a garnish of memory traces, and served to the starving or rejected mind of the individual. The child projects this image to a screen and perceives God after the pattern of the father. (Justice, 1984)

God is sometimes referred to as an existing physical being. He is all too often, the individual's imaginary private creation. Masculine gods are perceived as having a systematic, knowledgeable mind, and maintain infinite order. Feminine gods are more intimate. They will welcome the individual with open arms in a comforting, self-giving love. This image of God is not only seen as a physical entity, but forms a personality with assertive actions of regenerated emotions derived from parental role models. The communication breaks down when Jesus, who never married or had children, is presented as a loving God. The natural mind cannot comprehend a relationship with God different from that formed over the years with the natural parent, and without a system of acceptable works without faith. (Justice, 1984)

The Social Ministry

The Christian religion can be a threat to the essential security of an individual. This threat causes some anxiety resulting in calling out to others for help who, as yet, appear unconscious of impending danger. There are many anxious denominations, where Christians are preoccupied with many ministries. They come to Jesus asking, "Lord, do you not care that other Denominations left us to serve alone? Tell them to come and give us a hand." What was true for Martha, is true for the Christian Church; "You worry over too much ministry, when one ministry is all that is necessary." The church is threatened when administered by an ethical mind. A zealous Church will take on more, and be administered effectively, but with focus on the mandate for a social congregation.

Churches tend to focus on some symptom, while overlooking the real problem. Not long ago, it was sin for a woman to uncover her head. Now some women can uncover their entire body and show it to millions with little or no shame. Eve looked upon the Tree of Knowledge of Good and Evil, and it tantalized a symptom of lust. Her need for food and pleasure, backed up by the promise that she would be a little god, led her into rebellion. There was no thought given to the consequence of eating the fruit, but only on how it appeared on the surface. The Christian Church can meet all symptoms of society. Yet, there is a deeper spiritual symptom being overlooked.

A religious/political belief system determines the Church as a co-dependent. A co-dependent focus is on a dependents need for care. In November 1997 it was all about wearing a ribbon against pornography. This passion of co-dependency inspired a feeling of grandiosity among those who participated. Over the last four decades, Para-Church conferences held across North America show signs of a progressive co-dependent Church. It is so dependent on helping others outside the borders; it overlooks the need of those inside the walls. It is almost a form of militant fanaticism among the Christian community through which they justify a spiritual/

political power by working toward religious/social reform.

A former movement was the Miami Invasion of November 8-19, 1990. It was led by Larry Lea, and called "Warriors to Battle in Miami." This "Forceful Men Conference" held in Phoenix in August of 1990; and "Dominion '90" held July 29-August 3, 1990 advertised their meetings as follows: "Experience a return to Pentecost with a Fresh Militant Anointing! A less intense movement of the 90's, and still going strong, is the Promise Keepers. These are sincere Christian men committed to alleviating the moral decline of Church and family. These symptoms of Religion and Society, intensified by those who minister with religious/political fervor, is a threat to the unity of a functional faith based Church. Social reform is not the answer for unity, but a feeble attempt by a co-dependent Church in caring for a dependent society.

Learned people and scholars think, write, and speak, to these issues in the name of the Lord. History of the Christian Church shows how passion for the cause is required to maintain these religious movements. The Anabaptists, obsessed with the moral decline of their day, allowed passion to blur the vision for uniformity. In their zeal in dealing with the symptoms of society, they actually prepared for the millennial kingdom, and of Christ.

In the year 1535, the City of Munster, Netherlands, fell under the control of Jan Mathis and Jan van Leyden. These men claimed to be the anointed of God under the mandate of the Anabaptists. They taught that a militant force would bring in the Kingdom of God, and through coercion, others would join their movement or leave the city. Thousands of Anabaptists flocked to Munster in anticipation of Christ's setting up His Kingdom on earth.

Their dream of Christ returning to reign, as Prince of Peace became a nightmare as they observed Jan van Leyden crowned as King David ruling with an iron hand and instituting polygamy. A battle broke out and most of the city's inhabitants were slaughtered. Their hope for the Kingdom of God dissipated amid the violence. This was the effect caused by the passion of a caring co-dependent Church that turned out to be a religious/political anarchy.

History cautions the Christian Church about works. If motivated by an unbalanced obsession in bringing about the Kingdom of God, it results in social chaos. These modern day movements are no different. The Christian Church is too impatient. Again, James the brother of Jesus explains how the testing of faith results in patience, but to let patience be a work of maturity in, and for the Christian. (James 1:3-4) History shows how obsession over the Kingdom of God on earth and the symptoms of society, bring about religious/political insurrection, anarchy, and that by a co-dependent pattern of world Churches.

The Emerging Pattern

Christians who are obsessed with the idea that faith without works is dead places a false guilt within them. The call is no longer a request for help, but a call for believers to come out from all Churches, lest they partake of the sin of passivity, and incur the wrath of

God. Any, who are babes in Christ, or new converts from evangelistic, holiness, or charismatic meetings, hear these dispelling words, and not discerning the voice of the Holy Spirit, come as sheep for the slaughter. It is no longer, Jesus I need help, but Jesus let us represent you on planet earth, and we will pattern the will of the Lord upon the nations. This is coercive and detrimental to the cause of Christianity, and sets the stage for religious/political anarchy.

The Conditions

Delegated authority on God's jurisdiction is a conditional focus. Conditions are patterned so the Church may become obedient. All living creatures, formed out of the ground, were brought to Adam for naming. None of like kind was given for Adam. In obedience to God's will, Adam fell into a deep sleep. A rib was taken from his side, out of which, God made him a woman, a helpmate. The first husband/wife team, created and placed in the Garden of Eden, is an example of God's authority over His jurisdiction. (Genesis 2:19-24) Adam was God's delegated authority and Eve was the measurement of his authority.

God showed Adam what was necessary for marriage. Adam and Eve set the example for marriage. There was a condition given by which a man may leave his father and mother and take a wife. He must be obedient and willing to give of his life. Jesus was obedient to God and gave His life for His Bride the Church. A man, when obedient to God, will give his life for his woman, his vessel to honor and uphold her before the Father.

A husband becomes God's delegated authority for the wife. It has a condition. Husbands must love their wives as one flesh, for in marriage, two are made one. Parents are the delegated authority for their children. This also has a condition. They shall not provoke their children, but bring them up in the discipline and admonition of the Lord.

Employers are the delegated authority for their employees. Yes, with a condition. Employers must not manipulate by threatening to bridle their employees as if they were a horse or mule. The same condition applies to the employee. Both are under the authority of God. Intimidation should never control the work place. Political rulers are the delegated authority in relation to their subjects, but with a condition. (1 Corinthians 15:28) They are to govern impartially, without listening to those who would seek preference over others, but with justice and care for the poor, set the example. (Nee, 1972) The Christian is to lead a quiet and peaceable life in all godliness, virtue, and honor, in the sight of God, and under His delegated authority, is given political rule. (1 Timothy 2:1-5)

A Christian should not seek a political office. There are no guidelines in the New Testament giving instruction on how to be a political leader. As far as the Old Testament is concerned, Israel was under the authority of God until they demanded a King. (1 Samuel 10:17-25) Kingdoms of this world are under the jurisdiction of the devil. In the temptation of Jesus, the devil offered Him all the kingdoms of the world, and the glory that comes from a political office. (Matthew 4:8; Luke 4:6) A political office and the glory thereof, is an authority delegated to a non-believer. In 2008, we see professing Christians in the United States and Canada voted out of office in preparation for the new world government.

Unbelievers rule with knowledge, allotted to all mankind, of the tree of the knowledge of good and evil. They are enabled to judge between right and wrong. The pattern for guidance, judgment, and balance emerges from these two principles. Upon proper allegiance, these will suffice in the establishment of social stability. The Christian Church is not responsible before God in bringing social/political reform through some religious ethic. That is why Church and State are each held accountable before God in respect to jurisdiction. A loving and caring God has set this pattern for all mankind. Political reform, under the banner of a co-dependent Christian Church, or an egotistic Christian, is an example of deliberate disobedience.

The Better Portion

Christians are preordained to rule in the millennial Kingdom of Christ on earth. (Jude 1:14-15) Concerning existence, Christians are currently joint-heirs of the Kingdom of God in heavenly places in Christ. (Romans 8:17-29) Life in resurrection implies that the new creature in Christ does not exist in the flesh, but in the reality of the Spirit. (Romans 8:7-11; Galatians 5:17)

Many Christians are confused with their position in Christ. Pastors use the term (positional) to describe being in Christ. This is a mental attitude in which one stands: One takes this position, because of the nature of sin in the flesh. The term, "in Christ" is controversial. We cannot be in heaven and on earth at the same time. If we are "in Christ" in heaven, the condition is spiritual. If God raised Christ from the dead, and sits at the right hand of God, then we too, are raised from the dead in Christ, and sit in heavenly places. (Ephesians 2:6)

Many live after the flesh, hoping to please God. The truth is, because of righteousness, a better portion is allotted to us. (Romans 8:10) The principle of the knowledge of good and evil, right or wrong lay innate in Adam's posterity. Christians, who follow after the flesh, and seek political office, exercise a religious ethic. They assume the power of delegated authority granted only to the unbeliever.

Authority, in the will of God, is set apart as holy. It is not an attribute taught within most Churches. To represent authority is to represent God; to be in authority is to be an example to all. (Nee, 1972) Jesus gave the example of the vine and the branch. The Christian can do nothing outside of Christ. The Christian, who walks in the Spirit are under the authority of God. They are co-laborers together in Christ. (John 15:4-19; 17:9-16) The better portion of what a Christian can experience is to listen and be at rest in Christ Jesus. To listen, study, and meditate upon His Word, is the means whereby He ministers through the Spirit. The better portion of Grace is the adoration of God in the believer.

The Abuse and Loss of Authority

The abuse and loss of authority became real after the

Scopes trial in Dayton, Tennessee in 1925. The right to teach evolution over creation in the public school system became an issue when John T. Scopes rebelled against a State Law that denied him the right to teach evolution in his school's science class. William Jennings Bryan, an eloquent Presbyterian elder three times a candidate for the Presidency, led the prosecution. Clarence Darrow, who defended Scopes, lost his case to Bryan. However, teaching evolution in the classroom nevertheless soon spread across North America. This is an example of disobedience to undermine the authority of God. Bill 908 in California was debated as to the right of same sex marriage. The Bible is no longer the authority on things pertaining to society and politics. The Christian Church, in its abuse of authority, lost the battle between creation and evolution, and soon, the marriage bed.

Modern Theology carries the mark of evolution. A faith of works, not the work of the faithful, developed over eons of time. Is God yet able to bring about salvation to man? Does salvation depend on the death, burial, and resurrection of Christ? The Liberal Church seeks humanity's perfection. Suited after the design and pattern developed through the process of evolution, the Evangelical debates over who holds the key to Grace. The debate goes on with fifty seven percent of the evangelical church in favor of modern theology.

Tolerance is the focus in discerning works over faith. Seeking identity in a theological ethic, be it Arminian, Calvinism, Liberalism, Fundamentalism, or some form of Conservatism, is an issue for reform. There is agreement under the authority of God. When Christianity becomes tolerant of Islam, humanism, ethics, and debate, it results in a union leading to rejecting God's authority in society. Unity between the Church and State is highly improbable, but then again, where does regulation end? Let's not put the cart before the horse by altering the pattern of God's authority. It will only bring greater anarchy. The next chapter speaks further to God's authority. His Word, the Written Word, speaks to those called faithful in Christ.

Now you see it; then you don't. This chapter showed the church trapped under a social banner. With many non-church organizations springing up all over the world, the church seems to have forgotten her mandate to preach the gospel. Now you know why leaders have emerged to take up the cause under a socialist banner. The church is becoming a deregulated, conformist, and tolerant of social reformists. The faith of the fathers is placed under the table. Works, rather than faith, have taken the reins, and the church is being taken over by radicals. When revival happens, which is the title of the next chapter; you will see how the message of faith comes to the rescue.

CHAPTER NINE

WHEN REVIVAL HAPPENS

The Message

Being constrained of the Lord, this book is written to the Saints, and the faithful in Christ. Whereas, revival began in the grave, and lives again in resurrection, this chapter opens the door to Eternal Life. A revival is an awakening of no equal proportion. The Holy Spirit emerges in power, and is awakened in resurrection. Revival, as predicted in the Book of Hosea Chapter 6, Verse one, two, and three, provides the how, who, what, why, and the where of salvation. Unconditional love emerges in those who are faithful in Christ. Revival brings together brothers and sisters in the Lord. A common bond of communion among friends and comrades is the effect of revival.

The Scripture used religiously for revival is found in Second Chronicles Chapter Seven Verse Fourteen. It reads, "If my people, which are called by my name, shall humble themselves, and pray, and seek my face, and turn from their wicked ways; then will I hear from heaven, and forgive their sin, and will heal their land." Although written to Solomon for the sake of Israel concerning the temple, it is a message for today's Christian. The temple, spoken for religious worship is not of human hands, but a habitation of God through the Spirit. It was for this cause that Paul is called the prisoner of Jesus Christ for the Gentiles. (Ephesians 2:21-22; 3:1)

Israel became a Nation in 1948. Since that year, there have been external and internal struggles over who owns the Land of Palestine, and the Temple mount. Israel's occupation of the land is a threat to religious and political restoration. Wars and rumors of wars run wildly among surrounding nations. Ownership and occupation go hand in hand. It is an ongoing struggle for dominion.

The Christian struggles in much the same way. There is an external and internal battle as to ownership of our body. The external way of doing church in the sight of others is to oppose the internal spiritual journey of resurrection and the Cross. Confession of present and past sin becomes a contentious issue. Confession is necessary to repentance, but if it does not relate to the other, what is the advantage?

Revival begins with a struggle for ownership. It is not judicially imparted or positional imputed as an attribute of recognition. Revival is the experiential appropriation of bringing the power of resurrection into the reality of a new Life. The average good living Christian becomes a vital link in witness to the world of a Kingdom based in heavenly places. This message is to the Christian: "Do not stand in the world giving testimony to Christ, but stand in Christ, and give testimony unto the world." We are the children of God in Christ Jesus. We are His temple; He is our God, all that we have belongs to a merciful redeemer.

The Right to Ownership

To use force or coercion is the result a deceitful mind. Taking possession with acceptance, results in a spiritual fit. After we trust God for salvation, the Holy Spirit takes management. Repentance and sin are under the blood, and we accept the gift of faith. We are saved from the bondage and slavery of sin. The work of the Holy Spirit brings confirmation that the old is dead and buried; exchanging the chains of darkness for the freedom of light, we pass from death unto life; taken captive by His will, we ascend to heavenly places. In Christ, there is no disputing the right of ownership. Eternal Life is Christ's Life. (Colossians 3:4) When the Christian comes out from under the shadow of self, and acknowledge the ownership of God, there is an awakening to new life in resurrection. This is according to the working of the Lord.

God chose the concept of death to bring to nothing those who think they are all sufficient. Self cannot be magnified in His presence. God is omnipresent. It is through God's grace we are placed in Christ's death, wherein He is made unto us Wisdom, and Righteousness, and Sanctification, and Redemption. (1 Corinthians 1:30) He is all these and more. Christ is the giver and the gift of Eternal Life. Undeniable agreement is that His Life is Eternal.

Eternal Life shows God's ownership. There is no righteousness in the flesh, but there is the knowledge of good and evil. Most know what is good, and what is evil, but of sin very few know of its power to do, or not to do in the flesh. (Romans 7:17-18) The Gospel of John tells us that if one believes God gave us over to His Son in death, then whosoever believes God cannot perish, but has Eternal Life. Christ's Life, which is Eternal Life, is owner and operator, and whose giver is God. (John 3:16)

The Pretence

Pastors and Evangelists preach Christ's redeeming work for the sake of humanity. Many overlook the significance forgiveness has over past, present, and future sin. They advocate, on behalf of the church and of their office, for acts of sin in need of confession. Let us get this one defining fact clear. After confession and repentance of sin, we are set free from that body which put us under judgment. (Romans 6:6) There is no pretence here. The truth of the matter is we are made servants of the righteousness of God in Christ. (Romans 6:18) Cleansed from all unrighteousness, there is no further prescription for sin, but a description of grace. (1 John 1:9)

Therefore, the great commission is to go and teach all nations, baptizing them in the name of the Father, and of the Son, and of the Holy Ghost. (Matthew 28:19-20; Mark 16:15; Luke 24:47) The mode of baptism is to dip, to place, to immerse into Christ. Church baptism is in identification that the Christian is placed into Christ's death. (Romans 6:3-4) Some denominations are under the pretence that baptism places one into church membership, and thus secures eternal life. This implies only church leaders have the right to baptize. The command is to all Disciples of Christ. This is inclusive to all believers. The Christian is complete in Christ, anything less would nullify the significance of Water Baptism for identification.

The Creation of Life on Earth

Pastors, who teach a community of believers a factual interpretation of the Bible for Creation, reject the teachings of evolution. These pastors are Creationists. The pastor who teaches the first eleven chapters of Genesis as factual, are Creationists. They believe that life on earth was wrought through the Power of God.

One pastor in particular asked a visiting evangelist that he share the significance of the Genesis account as factual. The evangelist's response was negative. He claimed the creationist message would split the congregation and the clergy. (Ham, 1991) Christians should not be denied the right to hear the factual interpretation of the Bible. The idea that the Creationist message is deceitful, and divisive to the message of the gospel in building the Church, shows that compromise is a disease of epidemic proportion. If God is robbed of ownership, then His Word and Authority over His creation is lost. This is the epitome of greed, and society will pay dearly.

The Gift of Calling

Those who answer the call to ministry as an Evangelist, Pastor, or Teacher, exercise their respective office out of the same spiritual gift, the gift of prophecy. Disciplines in Christian education integrate the Body of Christ. While the world disciplines segregate its populace into different categories, the Body of Christ remains an integrated community of believers. The ploy of humanism in ministry is to stand above all without reproach, but the plan of God is that we stand in the unity of the Spirit giving testimony to the world. If the events of Genesis are not accepted as truth, it is highly unlikely an awakening will ever happen. The events in the Genesis account are critical to the birth, crucifixion, and resurrection of Jesus Christ. Any person, who denies the Geneses account, and the teaching of original sin, is deceiving the community of believers. The call of ministry must be divine at its source.

The Twentieth Century Awakening

Despite all that has been said, let God be truth and every man a liar. Revival remains firm, and assures victory for any Christian who seeks eternal life in Christ. Revival, in the City of Abbotsford, B.C., Canada, happened in the fall of 1969. In a furniture store, that sold rugs and drapery, a man came rushing into the store weeping. Upon seeing the owner, he went to him on his knees begging forgiveness. He had experienced an awakening, and was making restitution by restoring his trust with those he had done wrong. The first sign of revival is repentance.

The reward of true repentance is the peace of God. This chap had contracted with the storeowner, and upon leaving his position, stole business away through leeching customers. This man evidently knew, from some internal prompting, that he transgressed another Christian brother. Repentance brought peace through reconciliation, an experience that confirms love among the brethren.

On October 13, 1971, Ralph and Lou Sutera were led of God to Ebenezer Baptist Church in Saskatoon, Sask., Canada. One hundred sixty-five people gathered on a Wednesday evening for what many expected to be a routine series of meetings. A carload from Abbotsford and Prince George came to give testimony of what God was doing in their lives. (Lutzer, 1976) On January 7, 1972, these same revival fires spread to Vernon, then south to Kelowna before going on to Vancouver. Canada was experiencing a Christian awakening by the authority of God through repentance. Making restitution between brothers and sisters, God made provision for grace to abound, and abound it did!

Revival spread across Canada in the year of 1969. It spread unto many Nations across the world. In Denver, Colorado, Dr. Charles Solomon began a counseling ministry. He felt called of God to design drawings that illustrated scriptural truth. He developed a model for spiritual counseling, known as Spirituotherapy. This method is a registered copyright under the banner of Grace Fellowship International, and used exclusively by Dr. George Somerville, D.Phil.

On December 20, 1971, twenty-five men met prayerfully to discuss the possibility of opening an office for Revival Ministry in Canada. It was September 13, 1972, when Henry Teichrob, Gordon Dirks, with Robert Thompson, a Member of Parliament for Red Deer, Alberta, formed the first Canadian Revival Fellowship office out of Regina, Saskatchewan. (Lutzer, 1976) Twelve years later, a group of ten men approached The Canadian Revival Fellowship to have Ralph and Lou Sutera set up a series of meetings in Kamloops, B.C. A date was set and the first meeting began in the Alliance Church. As time went by the Holy Spirit began to convince men and women, boys and girls of sin in their life. Thus, the Flames of Freedom began to spread like wildfire across the North American Continent.

Harold Vaughan, Montvale, Va. began a Christ Life Ministry, and Neil Anderson's seven steps to Victory in Christ influenced thousands. This is just the tip of the iceberg that moved upon the Christian Community in the latter part of the twentieth century. This book, whose author was among the thousands who identified with Christ in 1984, is in anticipation of being an influence toward a twenty first century world awakening. Amen!

Summary

Now you know, that when revival happens, people repent and are baptized into the death of Christ. It follows then, that if baptized into His death, you are buried, and raised again to new life in Christ. (Romans 6:3-6) Revival, throughout this book, is seen as resurrection glory. My motive is to have you so moved that you would have fellowship in this cause. This cause is for the return of faith to its rightful owner, the Lord Jesus Christ in glory.

As you can see by the references there are many who take up the cross daily and follow Christ unto His death. Paul spoke strongly of this in Philippians, and with that I say , Good Day!

> ***"That I may know him, and the power of his resurrection, and the fellowship of his sufferings, being made conformable unto his death; If by any means I might attain unto the resurrection of the dead. Not as though I had already attained, either were already perfect: but I follow after, if that I may apprehend that for which also I am apprehended of Christ Jesus." (Philippians 3:10-12)***

REFERENCES

Beasley, Joseph D. (1987) Wrong Diagnosis, Wrong Treatment: (Essential Medical Information Systems, Inc.

Benton, Arthur and Pearl, David, Ed.,(1987) Dyslexia: An Appraisal of Current Knowledge, (London: Oxford University Press.

Brutten, M., Richardson, S. O., and Mangel, C. (1973) Something's Wrong with My Child: A Book about Children with Learning Disabilities. New York: Harcourt Brace Jovanovich. (pp 5,11)

Cairns, Earle, (1996) Christianity Through the Centuries, Third Ed., Zondervan.

Collins, Joshua, (2008) The Knowledge of Good and Evil, Post-Gutenberg Books, GlobalEdAdvancePRESS.

Canadian News release, November 24, 1997

Eliany, Marc, Ed. (1989) Report Alcohol in Canada, (Qttawa, Ontario: Health and Welfare Canada.

Emmett, C. V. (1978) Rx for Learning. p16.

Ericson, Edward (1988) The Humanist Way.

Forsander, Olof A. (1998) Effects of Ethanol on the Liver. Journal of Studies on Alcohol, Vol. 59,

Fried, Peter, (1983) Pregnancy and Life Style Habits, (Toronto, Ontario: General Publishing..

Ham, Ken, (1991) Genesis and the Decay of the Nations, (Creation Science Foundation Ltd.,Brisbane. Australia, Master Books Publishers, El Cajon, CA.

Justice, William G. (1984) Personalities of God, OGS Dissertation.

Ladies Home Journal, (1984) excerpt, February, "When Smart Kids Cant Learn."

Lazenby, Henry, OGS Classroom notes..

Lecky, W. E .H. (1883) A History of England in the Eighteenth Century (New York: 7 Volumes), Vol. 1,

Levinson, Harold (1994) Smart But Feeling Dumb. Warner.

Lutzer, Erwin W. (1976) Flames of Freedom, Moody.

Martin, Sara Hinds, Silent Shame, (1987) Westchester, Illinois: Crossway Books.

McConkey James H. (2005) The Threefold Secret of the Holy Spirit,

Miller, James G. (1978) Living Systems , New York: McGraw-Hill.

Money, John, (1962) Reading Disability (Baltimore, Md: The John Hopkins Press.

National News Coverage, (1997) December.

Nee, Watchman, (1972) Spiritual Authority.

Schaeffer, Francis (1976) A. How Should We Then Live? (Fleming H. RevellCompany, Old Tappan, New Jersey.

Solomon, Charles R., (1971) Handbook to Happiness, Tyndale House Publishers, Inc.

Swindoll. Carles R., (1992) Laugh Again, (1992) Word Inc., Dallas, TX,

Tuke, D.H. (1882), Chapters in the History of the Insane in the British Isles, Londra, Kegan.

U.S. News, (2008) June 23, http://religions.pewforum.org/ reports

Vaillant, George E. (1993) The Natural History of Alcoholism, (Cambridge, Mass: Harvard University Press.

Velton, Emmett and Simpson, Carlene T. (1978) Rx for Learning Disability, (Chicago:Nelson-Hall,.

Wadstein, Jan and Ohlin, Hans. (n/d) Changes in Water, Serum Electrolytes and Basic Acid Balance in Alcoholism.

Young, Warren C. (1963) A Christian Approach to Philosophy, Baker Book House, Grand Rapids, Michigan.

IS THERE REALLY LIFE AFTER DEATH?

The Believer's Identification with Christ
in His Death, Burial, and Resurrection.

ISBN 978-1-935434-35-1

an imprint of
GlobalEd AdvancePress

www.ingramcontent.com/pod-product-compliance
Lightning Source LLC
LaVergne TN
LVHW010100110826
845155LV00028B/430

* 9 7 8 1 9 3 5 4 3 4 3 5 1 *